Feng Shui Life Mapping

Feng Shui Life Mapping

Salvatore Manzi

TABLE OF CONTENTS

OUTLINE OF CONTENTS

Foreword

By Sivan Garr

Feng Shui Life Mapping is nothing short of miraculous. Salvatore has expertly woven together thousands of years of ancient Chinese knowledge and the popular art of Vision Boarding. Step by step, this book conveys these principles in such a clear and inspiring way, everyone can understand and apply the information immediately.

This has opened up an entire new world of how to create my life the way I want. Feng Shui Life Mapping begins with our defining our truly accurate intentions and goals, those that precisely reflect our innermost desires. Salvatore then describes how to manifest these goals in a very simple, yet compelling, direct and totally fun way. And the result is creating a fool-proof map to our personal future!

My own experimenting with Feng Shui Life Mapping started very simply. Salvatore suggests in addition to creating a Life Map, we use Feng Shui principals on every level of our environment: from our entire home down to our desktop. I decided to start with my desktop. It is where I spend the most time, so I felt I could easily practice what I learned and observe its effectiveness.

In the upper right hand corner of my table, I kept a full box of Kleenex. In my work, Kleenex is important to always have close at hand. Yet, after Salvatore explained that that corner was the Love & Partnership corner, I thought maybe a box of Kleenex was not the brightest thing to keep there! I promptly removed it. And, sure enough, I immediately felt an increased lightness and fun about my relationship. Almost as if an imperceptible cloud had been removed.

Eagerly, I began creating little changes all over my house, by strategically placing fresh flowers, or rose quartz, or leaving an area empty, to be open to new things! Transformations began happening everywhere and I was hooked.

As a spiritual teacher I work with people to heal their mind, emotions and their spirit. As a part of this, I believe that in order to have the life of your dreams, every area of your life needs to be addressed on your healing path from physical health, to relationships, to finances. Creating a well-rounded approach to healing is essential in order to sustain long lasting changes and improvements.

In my endeavors, I have always been attracted to Feng Shui as the "missing piece." The piece of the puzzle that teaches people how to create the support and clarity they need in their lives through the external world of their home and work spaces. My search led me to hire a few Feng Shui consultants. And, while I always felt the advice was clear and accurate, I never felt I walked away with any personal knowledge of the subject. I never felt that I had been given any tools I could at any time apply towards improving my life.

Salvatore's Feng Shui Life Mapping provided the missing puzzle piece! He has given us the teaching that not only allows us to improve our spaces, but to visually use our space and our Life Maps in order to create the life we always dreamed of having!

Feng Shui has become a part of my daily existence, which is something I always wanted. In addition, my Feng Shui Life Map has become a center focal point of my day! It took three tries before I created one that reflected to me exactly what I wanted. It is beautiful, inspirational and keeps me uplifted about my life and goals. Many doors have opened in my life that are in direct alignment with my personal Life Map.

I have no doubt that you will find a treasure of tools in this book! I encourage you to start using the principals right away and reap the wonderful results that you too will experience!

Sivan Garr, Spiritual Teacher, www.SivanGarr.com

How to Use This Workbook

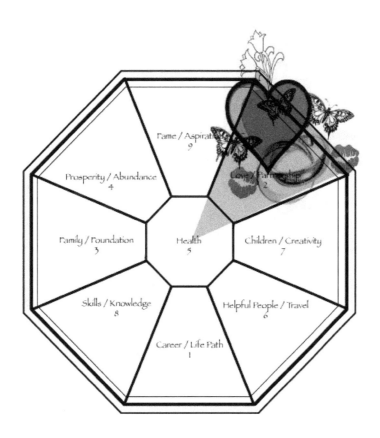

Fame / Aspirations
9

Prosperity / Abundance
4

Love / Partnership
2

Family / Foundation
3

Health
5

Children / Creativity
7

Skills / Knowledge
8

Helpful People / Travel
6

Career / Life Path
1

This book shares the secrets to manifesting your dreams. I have tried and practiced various fields of metaphysical studies, and this workbook is the culmination of my studies, intended as a guide for you to a competent understanding of these practices. As you work your way through, particular practices may resonant strongly with you and inspire more in-depth research and experimentation. Go for it!

Ideally, follow the workbook from beginning to end. Once you feel competent in creating CLEAR Intentions and SMART Goals, you may choose to do chapters 5, 6, and 7 to create a new Feng Shui Life Map for different stages of your life.

There are two ideal paths for working through this workbook: the **Short-Term Path** and the **Long-Term Path**, and you are welcome to create your own time line as well.

The Short-Term Path: ONE WEEK!

This path focuses on short-term intentions and goals and is ideal for learning and developing the practice of manifesting desired realities through Feng Shui Life Mapping.

- Commit to one hour of uninterrupted time per day for one week.

- Read and complete one whole chapter and the accompanying exercises each day.

- On day seven, you'll read chapter 7 and then make a collage as described in part IV.

The Short-Term Path emphasizes setting simple, short-term intentions and goals for your life. Hold the intention of creating a Feng Shui Life Map of what you would like for your life to look like in one month. The deadline for your goals is one month. So, what would you like for your life to **realistically** look like one month from today?

I recommend following the Short-Term Path a number of times, once a month or a quarter or a few times a year. The process will become familiar, and your successful use of a Feng Shui Life Map will become easy and consistent. Once you experience regular success with the Short-Term Path, it's time to follow the Long-Term Path.

The Long-Term Path: TWO WEEKS!

This path focuses on long-term intentions and goals and is ideal for those already familiar with the Law of Attraction (see chapter 1) or who have had success on the Short-Term Path. This path goes deeper into self-awareness, exploring our life's purpose while creating our ideal life.

- Commit to 1–2 hours of uninterrupted time per day for two weeks.

- Day 1: Read and complete the exercises in chapters 1–2

- Day 2: Read and complete the exercises in chapters 3–4

- Days 3–11: Each day, focus on one Life Area as described in chapter 5, using worksheets from chapters 2 and 3 to create

  - THREE CLEAR Intentions for one Life Area, each with

  - ONE long-term SMART Goal, that also has

  - ONE short-term SMART Goal

- Day 12: Read and complete the exercises in chapters 6–7

- Day 13: Allow yourself 2 hours to create a Long-Term Feng Shui Life Map as described in part IV

- Day 14: Create one Reflection in each of the Nine Life Areas of your home or office space

In completing the Long-Term Path, you'll be giving yourself permission to devote an hour each day for nine days to fully developing your long-term goals in each of the Nine Life Areas. Long-term goals can be for one year, five years, or lifelong. For your first Long-Term Path, it's probably best to start with a one-year deadline for your goals.

Ideally, you can use the Long-Term Path once a year either on your birthday or as a New Year's celebration to create a one-year Feng Shui Life Map.

Creating a Reflection is described in chapter 2 and is essential for activating your Map!

Create your own Path: Self-Paced!

There's always room for flexibility, and you may find it more useful to give yourself two weeks for the Short-Term Path, or one month to do the Long-Term Path. The important thing is to make a commitment to finishing the whole process, even if it's only a rough draft at first. To ensure this, sign the Statement of Intent at the end of the introduction.

Intention creates reality!

Introduction

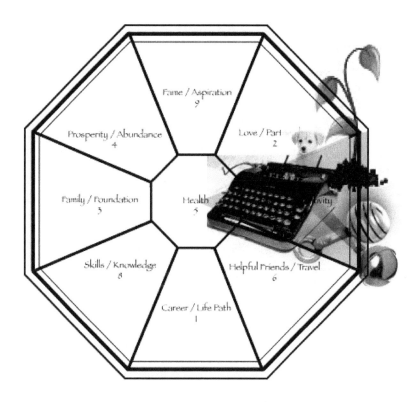

Fame / Aspiration
9

Prosperity / Abundance
4

Love / Partner
2

Family / Foundation
3

Health
5

Creativity

Skills / Knowledge
8

Helpful Friends / Travel
6

Career / Life Path
1

Your dreams are about to come true!

Prepare to manifest your dream life! Welcome to the exciting world of Feng Shui Life Mapping! You're embarking on an adventure that will transform your life! Amazing shifts and new realities are going to be quickly manifest as you apply the principles of Feng Shui Life Mapping to your life.

Clarify intention and create Reflection!

Your dreams start to come true when you follow two simple steps: (1) clarify intention, and (2) create reflections of your intentions. A Feng Shui Life Map does both by creating first a well-defined set of CLEAR Intentions for all Nine Life Areas of the Feng Shui Bagua and then a visual representation of those intentions in the form of a collage, called a Vision Board. It's that simple! Set a CLEAR Intention and create a Reflection in the form of a Visual Affirmation, and ba-da-boom, things start manifesting!

The images people choose for their Vision Board attracts unexplainable synchronicities in life. One such synchronicity happened to a first-time Feng Shui Life Mapper:

> *She placed the image of a golfer in the Prosperity & Abundance Life Area of her Feng Shui Life Map, and a week later, while passing by the President's Cup Golf Tournament, someone stuck some tickets through the fence and said, "Would you like free tickets to the Tournament? We have extra we can't use." She got to spend the next few days watching Tiger Woods play golf!*

Coincidence? What if I were to tell you that you can start creating these kinds of coincidences in your life regularly?! Free tickets worth hundreds of dollars is nothing compared with some of the things I've witnessed people create in their life!

Prepare for these kinds of phenomenal experiences! As you work your way through this workbook and begin using the powerful tool of Feng Shui Life Mapping, incredible synchronicities are going to begin happening in your life. And it all starts with a CLEAR Intention and a Reflection.

Informative and interactive, this workbook is divided into four parts.

Part I defines the metaphysical elements that combined create Feng Shui Life Mapping. Each element is worthy of its own book, and indeed there are many on the various topics! As your use of these elements increases, you create a foundation for manifesting all of your desires in life.

Part II explores the defining principles of creating CLEAR Intentions and SMART Goals, which is the heart of Feng Shui Life Mapping. The acronyms CLEAR and SMART lay out the process for creating clear and powerful intentions and goals, and you'll have a chance to practice each principle as you go.

Part III gives the Feng Shui Secret Formula to Life and how the practice of Feng Shui is specifically used for Feng Shui Life Mapping. Each chapter builds toward a complete and balanced set of intentions and goals that can be used as a foundation for creating a Vision Board and Feng Shui-ing one's space.

Part IV covers many of the basic fundamentals of applying Feng Shui to your Home and Office environment with suggestions as well as Feng Shui tips and tricks.

What is Feng Shui Life Mapping?

Briefly, a Feng Shui Life Map is a Vision Board built on the Feng Shui Bagua. A Feng Shui Bagua is a map depicting and dividing our lives into nine aspects, called the Nine Life Areas.

A Feng Shui Life Map starts by clarifying intentions and setting goals in all Nine Life Areas. Using Creative Visualization, these are developed into a Vision Board, which follows the map of the Feng Shui Bagua. Once completed, this Feng Shui Life Map can then be used as a guide, a blueprint, to create a supportive home and office environment that reinforces our intentions.

We can literally use it to create powerful reflections and visual affirmations of our intentions that serve to remind us of our dreams and keep our energies focused on manifesting them.

And once our Feng Shui Life Map has been completed and used to activate the energies of our environment, miraculous things begin to happen!

> *When I decided to move to Italy, I set my intention and created a reflection. I cut out images of Italy from a travel magazine and put them in the travel area of my home. Three months later, I had a job, a visa and an apartment waiting for me in Milan!*
>
> *The funny thing is that I had thought I'd like to live in Rome, but I got the job and apartment in Milan, and as I was taking down the photos from my wall, I noticed the fine print on them stating they were all*

photos of Milan. I had energetically drawn myself to
Milan!

Attitude

The importance of a positive attitude cannot be underestimated in the process of creating a Feng Shui Life Map. Skepticism is a natural and useful function in most aspects of life, but for creating miracles, it's best to discard any energies that would hold us back from dreaming big or would limit possibilities.

If nothing else, think of it as an experiment and engage a willing suspension of disbelief for one month. Just one month! Be open to the full breadth of this infinite universe!

Miracles are going to happen!

I've seen miracles happen again and again with people who create a Feng Shui Life Map. Throughout the book, I'll be sharing some of the real-life stories of amazing things that have happened in people's lives, such as the following story:

> *One client placed the image of an open door in her Career & Life Path Area, explaining that she wanted new opportunities to open up in her work life because she felt trapped in her position at work.*
>
> *When I visited her house, I noticed she had positioned her desk in her Career & Life Path, but it was facing the wall and pushed into the corner with part of the desk inaccessible because of the way the wall was sticking out. This arrangement had literally cornered and cut off her career!*
>
> *We turned the desk so that she faced the room instead of the corner, and a month later, she was transferred to a new department and placed in charge of the largest project in her company.*

Feng Shui

Feng Shui is an ART and a SCIENCE! It's the practice of living in harmony with the energetic vibrations of our environment.

The science of Feng Shui is based on the fact that all forms of matter are made up of energetic particles. These energetic particles emit vibrations, which by nature are attracted to, opposed to, and subject to cause and effect in relation to other vibrations. So the scientific aspect of Feng Shui is concerned with how the energetic properties of one particular element influence another element.

The art aspect of Feng Shui is similar to how we could call cooking an art. When we cook, we combine various elements in various quantities to yield various results. In Feng Shui, the idea is that by adjusting various energetic properties in our environment, we have the potential of yielding various energetic results.

To practice Feng Shui is to engage in balancing energetic vibrations and directing them toward supporting our highest intentions. To do this, our levers of control include not only our physical environment (such as the couch, the pictures, and the lighting) but also our mental and emotional environment (our thoughts, our feelings, our mental habits). In fact, when we start off our mental and emotional environment with the creation of a CLEAR Intention, we set into motion the most powerful force for the flow of energetic vibrations throughout our environment.

Feng Shui originated in ancient China. As the practice evolved over the centuries, different schools came into being. About five thousand years later, the practice made its way to mainland America in what is now commonly referred to as Westernized Feng Shui.

Feng Shui Life Mapping uses the Westernized practice of Feng Shui, using the Feng Shui Bagua as a guide to developing a complete and balanced set of intentions and goals for all Nine Life Areas. This then becomes the foundation for a Vision Board that can be used as a guide to "Feng Shui" one's space.

A Feng Shui Life Map can be used as a guide to creating reflections of your intentions throughout your home and office spaces. You may eventually wish to do a full Feng Shui Space Alignment to balance the many variable energetic forces to create harmony and ensure a supportive environment.

The options are limitless . . . the possibilities are infinite . . . and a new reality is just a thought away!

Statement of Intent

This Statement of Intent is here to ground and ensure that you use Feng Shui Life Mapping to its fullest. I would like to encourage you to fill this out, sign it, and post a copy of it somewhere that you'll see it regularly as a reminder of your commitment to this process.

I _____

do hereby state my INTENTION to create miracles in my life through the use of Feng Shui Life Mapping.

I commit to completing the following chapters and exercises of this workbook over the next _____ days.

My GOAL is to create a Feng Shui Life Map as a virtual representation and visual affirmation of my dream life.

My GOAL is to activate my Feng Shui Life Map by creating reflections of my intentions throughout my environment.

Signed: _____ Date: _____

PART I

Creating the Foundation

A new reality is
just one thought away!

CHAPTER 1

The Elements of
Feng Shui Life Mapping

This chapter discusses the basic elements of Feng Shui Life Mapping, the philosophical and metaphysical practices and teachings that unite to create this unique practice. Each element has volumes written to explore its profound insights and is worthy of the research and study each has inspired. Combing six essential practices, Feng Shui Life Mapping uses working with **intention** to direct **Chi**, the life force energy, to make manifest our every desire.

Feng Shui Life Mapping Defined

Feng Shui is the art of *Intentionally*
supporting the *Flow of Energy*
in all *Life Areas.*

Life Mapping activates the *Law of Attraction*
through the *Affirmation*
of a *Vision Board.*

Feng Shui Life Mapping uses the Vision Board
as a blueprint
to create an environment that reinforces
intentions and directs your life energies
to make manifest your dreams.

Feng Shui Life Mapping

Feng Shui Life Mapping combines a number of metaphysical practices into one comprehensive and powerful tool. The various practices can be divided into two categories: Feng Shui and Life Mapping.

Each category has three key elements. Feng Shui involves the use of Intention, the Flow of Energy or Chi, and the Feng Shui Bagua's Nine Life Areas. And Life Mapping involves working with the Law of Attraction, Affirmations, and Vision Boards.

Altogether, a Feng Shui Life Map is a **balanced** and **complete** visual **representation** of our life's aspirations. By nature of its being balanced, we have the opportunity to create a well-rounded and fulfilling life. As it's complete, we have a natural commitment to achieving our dreams. And as it's a representation of our life's aspirations on a Feng Shui Bagua, we are able to use it as a guide to easily create an environment that supports and affirms our intentions.

Let's discuss each element in more detail.

The Vision Board

A **Vision Board** (also known as a treasure map, goal map, goal board) is a collection of images, drawings, words, or any type of visuals in the form of a collage that expresses the ideas and ideals of our dream life.

A Vision Board is a collection of

> all the things we wish **TO HAVE**,
>
> all the things we wish **TO DO**,
>
> and all the things we wish **TO BE.**

The best use of a Vision Board is one that creates a balance between and incorporates all three aspects. However, many practices of Vision Boarding focus on just one. Such a focus leads to a life that's out of balance and ultimately unsatisfying. It's great to "have" a lot of things we desire, but if we're not "doing" what we wish to be doing, there's little joy in "having" things. And the same can be said of "doing" what we wish without "being" who we wish to be, or "being" who we wish to be but not "having" what we wish. For this reason, the practice of Feng Shui Life Mapping stresses the importance of creating a balance and incorporating all three aspects in each Vision Board that is created.

Some Vision Boards use quite specific images, and some use broad conceptual images: both create powerful results! Specific images are useful when we have a clear and specific idea of our ideal life. For example, if we wish to own a certain house, we could use a picture of that house. Broad images are useful in pointing us in a direction while leaving us open to specific possibilities. For example, if we wish to be in love, we can use the image of a heart.

The images we select direct our focus to begin finding and thus attracting us toward those realities and bringing them into our lives. We witness this type of activity when we begin thinking about something and then start to notice that thing more and more around us.

For example, one day my friend told me he was going on a cruise. He told me all about where it was going and what was on the board. He painted a clear visual **image** of the cruise. Later that day, I noticed some cruise advertisements in the window of a travel agency I was passing. Later, I found advertisements for cruise ships in a magazine I was reading. And then another cruise ship image popped up online while I was reading the news . . . and so on and so on.

This works in part because of the correlation between the conscious and subconscious mind. The subconscious mind sees what's **imagined** and believes that to be reality. The subconscious then directs the conscious mind to notice evidence of that reality more and more.

My subconscious mind had **tuned into** the image of cruise ships, and I began to see them everywhere I looked. The key here is that the images of cruises were already around me; they would have been there whether or not I noticed them. But my subconscious mind was tuned into looking for them and brought my conscious mind's attention to them.

The more we engage the subconscious in determining what is reality through imagining a desired reality or focusing on a particular image and imagining it as a part of our lives, the more the conscious mind begins to seek out that reality and to lead us to different places, situations, people that will ultimately create that reality.

The conscious mind confirms the
beliefs of our subconscious mind.

Vision Boards focus our attention and attract our conscious mind to the things we desire. The subconscious mind believes the reality depicted on the Vision Board and tunes the conscious mind to recognize any semblance of that reality, directing us, and our energies, toward that reality.

In this way, a Vision Board is a Visual Affirmation, which activates the Law of Attraction to begin making manifest our desired realities.

We'll discuss how to create a successful Vision Board, as well as how to activate it to begin manifesting realities, in chapter 7, but first let's talk about Affirmations and the Law of Attraction.

Affirmations

An affirmation is a statement focused on the **positive** aspect of life. There are always two sides to every coin! By working with affirmations, we are choosing to focus on the positive side.

An affirmation is also a **wish** stated as if it were already true. Sometimes an affirmation expresses our hope in the **positive potential** of any given situation. And sometimes an affirmation is a leap of faith.

Let me differentiate between faith and hope. Faith is believing in something when we're not sure it's even possible, whereas hope is believing that something we know is possible will happen in a way we're not sure it will. Affirmations bridge our faith and hope to our desired reality by focusing on the positive potential of the universe.

Affirmations activate the law of attraction to bring the positive potential into reality.

An affirmation is a special tool that seeks to create a new **thought-habit**, a new unconscious and automatic response to life. Biologically, whenever we think something over and over again, neurological connective tissue is laid down along that "train of thought." Over time, the thought becomes a habit that we no longer have to stop and think about, as our response becomes automatic.

If I were to ask you your name, you would immediately respond. You know your name. You don't have to think about it. If I were to ask you to tie the strings of a shoe, you wouldn't think about it, you would just do it automatically. Thought-habits are ideas, beliefs, values, and skills that are biologically circuited into our neural network and control our routine actions and responses.

Thought-habits can also form as a negative response to life situations. As we affirm these negative thoughts and thought habits, they become stronger and more automatic so that when approached with a situation, we have an immediate, unconscious negative response.

Ask someone to sing or dance or any number of other performance-related activities, and he or she may quickly respond, "Oh, no, I can't." They don't think about it: they've conditioned themselves to respond automatically because at some point in their lives they witnessed or experienced something embarrassing and then began reaffirming that negative thought again and again until it became an unconscious and automatic response.

An affirmation

- **creates a new thought-habit,**
- **breaks an old thought-habit,**
- **focuses on the positive,**
- **makes a wish on the positive potential!**

Affirmations short-circuit the neural connective tissue that was our automatic response. They force us to slow down and pay attention to our response, and CHOOSE a different one, a positive one!

Let's use the example of shoes and how automatic responses are made and broken. I don't think about putting my shoes on my feet, I just slip them on! But if I wanted to put on a pair of ski boots, I'd have to stop and give it some thoughtful attention. The habit of putting my shoes on easily, effortlessly, and automatically is short-circuited by the new boots. But, miraculously, after a few days or a week of skiing, a new thought-habit is formed, new neural connective tissue is laid down, and I no longer have to focus much attention on putting on the ski boots. It's a new automatic response, a new habit. It happens that fast!

An affirmation is like a ski boot. It breaks us out of the habit of simply, unconsciously putting on our shoes and gives us the opportunity to create something new. And if an affirmation is like a ski boot, Feng Shui Life Mapping is like Olympic downhill skiing! After some practice, you can achieve the Gold in anything you desire!

The Law of Attraction

The Law of Attraction is the driving principle of Feng Shui Life Mapping, Affirmations, and Vision Boards. The law states that we attract that which we direct our focus on, whether or not it's desired, as the law is indiscriminate. Scientifically, the law is based on the fact that all forms of matter are made up of energy, and energetic vibrations are attracted to similar vibrations: positive attracts positive and negative attracts negative.

Like attracts like.

The idea is that as we focus our minds on a particular reality, we magnetically begin to attract that reality into our lives because our conscious mind begins to notice any semblance of it and draws us to it.

And a Feng Shui Life Map gives us a balanced and complete concrete image to focus our minds on in order to start attracting a new life.

Create space for the new!

The Law of Attraction is at work at all times in all aspects of our lives. For this reason, many Feng Shui practitioners begin by emphasizing the need to **clear clutter** as well as any objects holding energetic vibrations of our past experiences that no longer serve us. Imagine the life we're attracting when clutter surrounds us!

When our environment is affirming, visually, a world of clutter, not only does it slow down, detour, and block new energies from flowing into our lives, but such an affirmation makes it difficult to break old habits, create new opportunities, and make the shifts necessary to manifest our desired realities.

We can't control the "how."

Often, when we wish to create a shift in our lives, we strive to figure out how to do it. We wrestle in our minds with all the possibilities, we make charts of pros and cons, we weigh options, and we drive ourselves insane in an attempt to assure ourselves of success. The Law of Attraction does not need to be micromanaged!!!

The best way to ensure success is to put the intention out into the universe and allow the universe to figure out how best to bring it into reality. Within no time of setting a CLEAR Intention, the universe will start to drop little synchronicities into your life and give you a heartfelt buzz to pursue such leads until . . . voilà! . . . the new reality is made manifest.

It's good to have a plan, keeping in mind that the best plan is open to unforeseeable opportunities, twists, turns, and miracles!

One step at a time!

Another aspect of the Law of Attraction that can be confusing at first is the lack of control over the timing.

The Law of Attraction works powerfully and quickly, but sometimes the shifts we're creating need to be made in tiny increments. Instant, immediate gratification just might happen, and I've witnessed it when people have simple CLEAR Intentions. However, the bigger the shift we wish to manifest, the more elements we need to allow time for realignment in order to create a successful shift. This patient, progressive shift prevents a whiplash effect of disillusionment or superficiality.

It's a cliché that Rome wasn't built in a day, but it's a good reminder to remain steadfast and to use the principles of SMART Goals (discussed in chapter 3) to allow small accomplishments to strengthen your commitment, gradually leading to the fulfillment of all your intentions.

I've witnessed what can only be described as miracles, with someone attracting into his or her life the exact items that they had put on their Vision Board or into the specific locations in their homes, with the intention of activating the Law of Attraction and manifesting that reality into their own lives.

> *One client had cut out the image of a sexy model and put it in her Love & Partnerships Area. A month later, she met him! Not just someone who looked like him, but the actual model. She sat down next to him in a coffee shop while on a business trip in New York City, and he started talking to her.*

The Law of Attraction is most effective when we have a CLEAR Intention and SMART Goals to follow toward affirming that intention. We'll discuss these principles in the next two chapters, but first let's summarize Life Mapping.

Life Mapping

Life Mapping is somewhat like gardening: planting a seed, tending it as it grows, harvesting at the right time to enjoy the fruits of our labor.

When a seed is planted, it begins to change both itself and its surroundings. It begins to **absorb** the water and nutrients around it. It's important to recognize that the nutrients were already there when the seed was planted, but the seed **attracted** these elements to it and used them to create something new.

When we create a Feng Shui Life Map, using Visual Affirmations to activate the Law of Attraction, we have planted a seed, we have set ourselves on a course, shifting our reality, attracting the necessary nutrients (which are already present all around us in this infinite universe) to make manifest that reality.

We can choose to accelerate this process by aligning the Visual Affirmations on our Vision Board with our actual environments, creating a **3-D Vision Board** in our home or office space that reinforces our intentions to speedily create new thought-habits, multiply the power of the Law of Attraction, and make manifest our dreams.

Feng Shui

Feng Shui, again, is the art of Intentionally supporting the Flow of Energy in all Life Areas. Let's discuss each of these key elements in more detail.

The Feng Shui Life Areas

Ancient Chinese Masters identified Nine Life Areas that need to be balanced, nurtured, and developed to create a fulfilling life.

These areas are (each area is described in detail in chapter 5)

- Career & Life Path
- Love & Partnership
- Family & Foundation
- Prosperity & Abundance
- Health
- Helpful People & Travel
- Children & Creativity
- Skills & Knowledge
- Fame & Aspiration

These Nine Life Areas are laid out on an octagon called a Feng Shui Bagua, with the eight sides and the center giving us the nine areas. In Westernized Feng Shui it's commonly depicted as an octagon stretched into a square, with a tic-tac-toe in the middle to give us the Nine Life Areas in more of a grid shape.

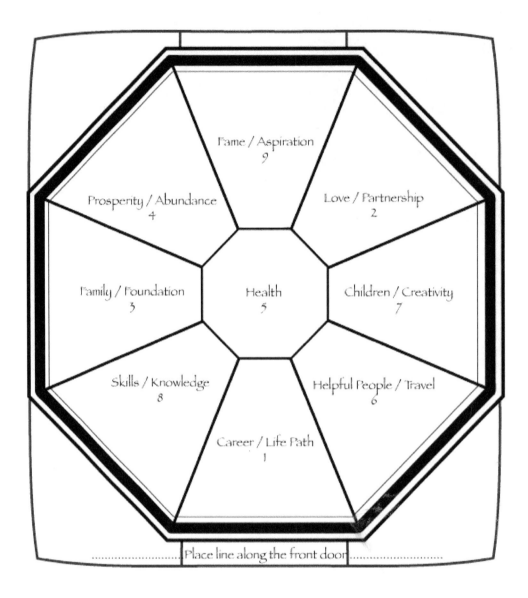

Fame / Aspiration
9

Prosperity / Abundance
4

Love / Partnership
2

Family / Foundation
3

Health
5

Children / Creativity
7

Skills / Knowledge
8

Helpful People / Travel
6

Career / Life Path
1

Place line along the front door

In Westernized Feng Shui, this Bagua can be placed over the blueprint of a home, a room, or an office space, lining the bottom of the Bagua up with the wall of the main entrance. In this way, you would always be entering the Skills & Knowledge, the Career & Life Path, or the Helpful People & Travel Areas.

If you have multiple entrances, the main entrance is the one to consider, even if it's not the one you use most often. One suggestion often given is to use the main entrance regularly even if it's more convenient to enter through the side or back doors of a space so that you're bringing good and fresh energy into the space.

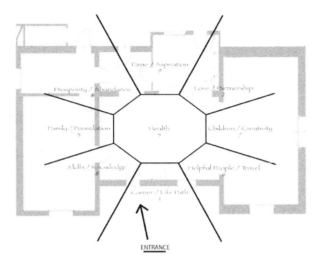

Consultants use the Bagua as a guide when they come to Feng Shui a space. It allows them to assess the physical space and determine what areas need to be focused on, enhanced, or adjusted to promote the changes desired.

Working without the limits of physical space, we're going to use the Bagua as a foundation for creating our ideal environment, our Vision Board, and that's why I call it a Feng Shui Life Map.

A Vision Board on a Feng Shui Bagua
is a Feng Shui Life Map!

And because your Life Map is built on the Bagua, you can take it home and use it as a guide to Feng Shui your space.

For example, by lining the bottom of the Bagua along the wall with the main entry, we can use the map to identify the area of your home that represents your Love & Partnership, the far right corner when you face the space from the front. And when we go to that area of your space we can look to see what in that area reinforces the intention you put down on your Life Map.

If you intend to be in a loving and healthy relationship, and there's a dead plant there . . . it has to go! And by placing a new, healthy plant in this area **with the intention** of it representing a healthy relationship, you're creating a visual affirmation that will begin attracting a new healthy relationship into your life. You're creating a new thought-habit. You're planting a seed, which the universe will feed and water through the universal flow of energy.

Flow of Energy/Chi Flow

The flow of energy of life, called "Chi" in Chinese, or "Prana" in Yogic language, or sometimes referred to as "breath of life" in Western society, is the energy that infuses us, and all living things, with life. Chi is constantly in motion and moves in and all around us at all times.

Feng Shui is the art of living in harmony with Chi.

Healthy Chi Flow is smooth and strong, easily spreading throughout our environment from where it enters to where it exits. Unhealthy Chi Flow is fast, erratic, or weak and creates disharmony as it gets stuck or stagnant or blocked.

There are several elements in life that influence our individual Chi Flow, including our constitution, actions, environment, and current events.

Four Influences on individual Chi Flow

- **our constitution**: our mental, emotional, and spiritual condition and conditioning

- **our actions**: including both proactive and reactive actions

- **our environment**: including objects, symbols, and other people

- **current events**: within our community, society, and the world

These influences on individual Chi Flow ebb and flow like the ocean's tides. The goal of Feng Shui Life Mapping is to create a clear direction for our individual Chi Flow so that we may remain balanced, directed, and at peace in the face of any circumstance.

Feng Shui Life Mapping successfully harmonizes these four influences of Chi Flow by working with them on two energetic pathways: Internal Chi Flow and External Chi Flow.

Two energetic pathways to work with Chi Flow

- External Chi Flow: the physical, tangible world

- Internal Chi Flow: the less-tangible world of our mental and emotional state

External Chi Flow is harmonized by working with the more-tangible world of our environment, the physical objects such as the desk, chair, sofa, walls, and windows, as well as physical influences of other people and current events. The external work of Feng Shui Life Mapping involves

- identifying and removing the **physical blocks** to Chi Flow

- enhancing Chi Flow with **Visual Affirmations** that reinforce our intentions (like the healthy plant)

Internal Chi Flow is harmonized by working with the less-tangible world of our constitution, our thoughts, emotions, and spiritual condition and conditioning, as well as the influences other people and current events have on our psyche. The inner work of Feng Shui Life Mapping involves

- identifying and removing the **mental and emotional blocks** to Chi Flow

- enhancing Chi Flow with **verbal and mental affirmations**

- setting **CLEAR Intentions and SMART Goals** to direct our individual flow of energy

Many clients are surprised when I come into their space and identify blocks in their personal lives by assessing their physical space. They think I'm some sort of psychic who's reading their aura or able to read their minds. But in reality, our physical environment reflects our inner world as much as it's influenced by it.

It's possible to Feng Shui a person's space to effectively direct a person toward a shift in a consciousness, but it's far more effective to begin with an internal shift and let that shift become reflected in his or her environment.

For this reason, Feng Shui Life Mapping begins by working with the Internal Chi Flow, starting by setting CLEAR Intentions and SMART Goals. From this foundation, necessary shifts in the physical environment become obvious, easy, and even FUN! And all this begins with intention.

Intention

Intention is the driving force of the energy that is and becomes our life. We're giving the ability to direct the universal flow of energy through the powerful tool of intention.

Energy flows where intention goes!

I liken the flow of energy to a breeze. It's invisible and enters into a space and begins to disperse throughout it. If the space is improperly aligned physically, the breeze may sputter around, or knock and stream through frantically.

The flow of energy is like the flow of water.

For a more tangible analogy, I liken the flow of energy to water: rain, streams, rivers, oceans . . . water is constantly in motion, as is the flow of energy. Water does not look for a specific path, it finds the path of least resistance and flows.

Intention is like using a hose to direct water. We decide how much, where, and with what force we wish to direct the water. We could also build a canal, or even a dam, to control and direct the water. In any case, the water continues to flow, as does energy. If water encounters a dam, it will create a lake, or in some cases a swamp, but eventually the water will build up and overtake the dam, or any obstacle, to continue on its path.

In a similar manner, energy is doing what it does naturally, flowing along the path of least resistance. And if it encounters a dam caused by physical obstacles such as the dead plant in our Love & Partnership Area or mental and emotional obstacles such as disharmonious thoughts and emotions, the energy will pool up to create a lake or a swamp.

However, if our intention is CLEAR, the flow of energy will continue and eventually overtake any obstacle. For this reason, whenever I work with a client, I like to emphasize that intentions are stronger than any obstacle.

Intentions are stronger than any obstacle!

For this reason I don't like to use the term "Bad Feng Shui," as I don't believe in such a thing. There may be misalignment, but perhaps that's the path we've chosen to take in order to encounter specific obstacles so as to strengthen and purify our intentions. Who am I to judge whether a person desires to go through some personal trial in order to learn some lesson he or she unconsciously or consciously feels is necessary before achieving his or her dreams?

There is no such thing as Bad Feng Shui!!!

We probably all know people who have a powerful ability to accomplish whatever they set their minds to, yet they live in an environment entirely counter to what most would consider "good Feng Shui." Their desks are full of clutter and their homes are awkward to move around in. But these are people who have learned how to focus their intentions as if using a laser beam, and through incredible self-discipline, strength, and willpower, push forth to their goals.

Feng Shui Life Mapping offers a less-difficult path. Feng Shui Life Mapping allows us to become aware of our intentions so that we can recognize where we have blocks and can then decide consciously whether to release them.

The key is in creating CLEAR Intentions. Once CLEAR Intentions are set, incorrectly aligned obstacles to Internal or External Chi Flow are easily overcome, and the Flow of Energy will move on to manifest whatever dream we can imagine.

Intention creates reality!

This is why Feng Shui Life Mapping starts with the inner work of creating CLEAR Intentions. We can choose to not adjust our physical space and still be successful in manifesting our dreams.

We have a choice:

- in deciding how fast we wish to manifest our dreams.

- of whether to become aware of and remove the obstacles, both internal and external.

- of whether to affirm our new reality and reinforce our intentions with verbal and visual affirmations.

By beginning this process, you're indicating your interest in creating your own reality. And just by reading these pages, you are setting in motion changes in your life, subtle and sometimes not so subtle, that will indeed lead to your manifesting your dream life.

And so, we're going to start this adventure with the inner work and get CLEAR on our Intentions. From CLEAR Intentions, we can then set SMART Goals. Using a powerful step in the art of Creative Visualization, we'll create a Vision Board that's a perpetual affirmation and virtual representation of a complete and balanced dream life.

With this map, this blueprint, we'll be able to easily perform the outer work of Feng Shui to create a supportive environment that reinforces our intentions and invites miracles into our life!

Review

Take a moment to explain, write out, and review the terms in bold.

Feng Shui is the art of *Intentionally*

supporting the *Flow of Energy*

in all *Life Areas.*

Life Mapping activates the *Law of Attraction*

through the *Affirmation*

of a *Vision Board.*

Feng Shui Life Mapping uses the Vision Board

as a blueprint

to create an environment that reinforces

intentions and directs your life energies

to make manifest your dreams.

PART II

CLEAR Intentions
Lead to SMART Goals

Think BIG
and celebrate
each small step!

CHAPTER 2

CLEAR Intention

Intention creates reality! In this chapter, you'll learn the principles for creating clear and powerful intentions, which become the driving force for directing life energies toward manifesting your dream life.

Once we distinguish the difference between Intentions and Goals, and start from a place of CLEAR Intention, our path becomes easy and fulfilling. CLEAR is an acronym describing the five principles for ensuring clarity with an intention, which are given here with specific tests to use as well as steps to improve your intention.

CLEAR Intentions lead to SMART Goals

The first step to creating your dream life is to set CLEAR Intentions about what you desire and, based on these CLEAR Intentions, to develop SMART Goals. CLEAR and SMART are acronyms outlining key principles for creating powerful intentions and goals. But first it's important to understand the difference between the two.

Many people use the two terms interchangeably, saying they "intend" to do something and "have a goal" of doing that same thing. But there is a difference! Once we understand the difference, and create clarity around intentions first, we begin to live a life full of success, possibility, and satisfaction.

Goals are the WHAT and Intentions are the WHY.

Simply put, goals answer the question "What? What is it that we wish to achieve?" And Intentions answer the question "Why? Why is it that we wish to achieve it?"

When we operate with awareness of our intention, we open ourselves up to a large array of goals to fulfill that intention, whereas if we operate only with an awareness of our goal, we are limiting our fulfillment to one particular future reality.

Intentions are the foundation on which goals are built, and goals are the specific future realities we envision will fulfill our intention.

To put it another way:

> Intentions are the driving force, which inspire and direct us to take action. For example, "I wish to take care of my body."

> Goals are the milestones we expect to pass along the way to fulfilling our intention. For example, "I will find a good restaurant," "I will choose a healthy meal," "I will feed myself."

In the next chapter on SMART Goals, we'll look at the importance of framing goals in a **Reaffirming** way: "I wish to take care of my body; therefore, I feed myself healthy meals in good restaurants." There are ways to select the best wording so intentions and goals become Reaffirming. For now, let's keep fleshing out the difference between goals and intentions.

Does the expressed desire have an outcome?
YES? . . . It's a Goal!

A quick way to tell the difference between intentions and goals is to ask if the desire you're expressing has a completion point. If it does, then it's a goal. A goal is focused on the future, an end point, or an outcome. Intentions don't have clear-cut end points, as they don't end.

For example, let's say my desire is "to have a car." Most people would express this as "I want a car." To figure out if this expressed desire is a goal or intention, we can ask whether it has a completion point. It does! Once we get a car, then it's completed. So it's a goal.

Knowing this expressed desire is a goal, we can then take a step back and ask ourselves, "WHY do I desire a car? What's my motivation? What intention does this goal honor?" The answer to those questions is the intention that inspired the goal. Perhaps the answer is that we wish to get to work easily, or have the ability to travel freely, or wish to create an image of ourselves as being sophisticated.

When I know my intention, I can set a whole range of goals to fulfill that intention **in addition** to getting a car. To have a sophisticated image, I could get a new wardrobe, hang out with particular friends, put up a profile on sophisticated.com. By first being clear about my intention and then creating a number of goals, I open myself up to a greater number of possibilities that I'll fulfill my intention whether or not I get a new car. In other words, I can begin and continue to experience fulfillment and satisfaction even before I get the car.

And that's the point! Awareness of intention leads to a fulfilling and satisfying life!

Goals are focused solely
on a particular future.

Having goals is good! We need them. Goals help provide direction to life, but as they are focused solely on one particular future reality, they don't help us deal with all the generalities of the present moment. Goals may not keep us motivated and directed as we encounter challenges along our path.

For example, in my job, if I'm not aware of my intention, but only know that I have a goal to get a certain promotion, I become focused on getting that promotion, and until I get it, I'm left unfulfilled. If something happens to delay my getting that promotion, I can lose my sense of direction, I can become frustrated, burned-out, and give up and stop trying. Giving up when we fail happens ONLY when we're unaware of intention.

A focus on intention will lead
to unlimited possibilities!

Now, if on that job, I understand that my intention, the foundation on which I have built the goal of gaining that promotion, is "to be recognized for my talents," then I open myself up to unlimited possibilities and will find a myriad of other ways to affirm my intention in addition to having the goal of getting the promotion.

I'll experience a greater potential for my intention being fulfilled because I'm not limiting the universe to just one particular way to fulfill it. Remember, with the Law of Attraction, we can't control the "how"! As we set intention, the universe begins to attract all the elements necessary to fulfill that intention.

Maybe my boss will say, "Thank you for your work." My intention is being fulfilled. I didn't set a goal of my boss saying that, but because I came from a place of awareness of my intention, I opened myself up to the universe finding and creating this experience to lead to affirmation of my intention.

Or maybe I'm placed in charge of a new project. My intention is being fulfilled. I didn't plan on or have the goal of taking charge of the project, but coming from a place of awareness of my intention led to the possibilities for that to happen to fulfill my intention.

I can still create any number of goals that I think will satisfy my desire to be recognized, but I'm not limiting the universe to fulfilling my intention in only one particular manner.

I can still have the goal of getting that promotion, but the universe will keep sending opportunities to affirm my intention along the way so that I'm not left frustrated or hopeless during the time I am striving for it.

Intentions hold direction
along the ever-changing flow of life.

Goals change! But if a goal is blocked, altered, or abandoned, we still have our intention, our direction, and can create new goals, remaining focused on fulfilling our desires.

Setting goals is necessary, but understanding the intention behind the goal will clear the path to experiencing fulfillment of our desires and allow us to maintain our direction in life no matter what happens along the path to realizing our dreams.

So, with the intention of creating clarity around our intentions, let's look at what makes an intention CLEAR and how CLEAR Intentions lead to SMART Goals!

Intention exercise

As we work through the principles of a CLEAR Intention, let's begin by coming up with one intention. Pick an area of your life from the Nine Life Areas as defined in Feng Shui and write down one intention that you have for yourself for that area. (Again, if what you write down can be checked off your to-do list, then it's a goal. If it's a goal, answer the question, "Why do I wish to accomplish this?" and that will lead to your intention.)

The Nine Life Areas again are

•   Career & Life Path

•   Love & Partnership

•   Family & Foundation

•   Prosperity & Abundance

•   Health

•   Helpful People & Travel

•   Children & Creativity

•   Skills & Knowledge

•   Fame & Aspiration

Write your intention here:

_____

_____

_____

Now, let's go through the principles of CLEAR and see how we can make your intention clear and powerful!

Conviction

A clear intention comes from a place of absolute conviction. It must be something we believe in 100 percent, without any shadow of doubt. It can't merely be daydreaming or wishful thinking of what we'd like to see in our lives somehow, sometime. It can't just be something we believe is the good and right thing for us because it's a value impressed on us by others in our life or by our community. It has to be something **we** believe is right for us and we believe has a genuine possibility for in our life.

It has to be something
that we believe!

A powerful test is to stand in front of a mirror and state the intention while looking directly into your eyes. Any hint of doubt will lead us to look away for a moment, look down, or prevent us from speaking with conviction.

Another way we can test the conviction that we have in our intention is by stating it out loud, to ourselves. As we do so, any doubts that we have will gurgle up in our minds, sometimes loudly and sometimes just as whispers.

The mind can't help but speak out all its fears in an effort to keep us from failing. Our mind wants to protect us from failure and disappointment, so it throws out all these challenges to stop us from making a mistake. But these challenges don't need to stop us! They merely provide insights as to where we have negative thought-habits. And remember, thought-habits can be changed, short-circuited, using affirmations!

If my intention is "to have a fulfilling job," but when I speak my intention aloud, my mind answers back, "You can't have a fulfilling job! No one has a fulfilling job! Look how your parents struggled! You don't deserve that!" Then I know my conviction is not 100 percent, and I need to first work on removing those doubts by developing affirmations to change my thought-habits.

When I hear a torrent of negativity, it's easy to get discouraged and give up. But I can use it to create clarity in my life. Instead of feeling discouraged, I can listen to the doubts bubble up and offer up thanks for the clarification! Now that the negative thoughts are exposed, I know exactly what's prevented me from already manifesting this reality in my life. The unconscious and automatic thought-habits holding me back no longer have the ability to operate secretly! I now know where I need to begin in order to clear a path toward manifesting my intention.

Conquer doubts using affirmations!

Make a list of all the doubts that come up about your intention and then write one affirmation for each doubt. Recite these affirmations daily for at least two weeks, and as you do, envision the affirmation being realized.

If my doubt is "no one has a fulfilling job!" my affirmation can be "I know people with fulfilling jobs!" And as I recite that affirmation, I can envision meeting people who tell me how much they love what they do, how much it fulfills them and excites them to do their work.

By combining my affirmation with visualization, I supercharge my activation of the Law of Attraction and begin to attract people into my life that do indeed enjoy their jobs. This proves my affirmation to be true. and before I know it, my doubt, that negative thought-habit, has been short-circuited and replaced by a new and powerful positive thought-habit about life, "People do have fulfilling jobs!"

Keep in mind that as we achieve clarity with our intentions, we manifest our desires, so it doesn't matter how long it takes to eliminate all our negative thought-habits as long as we continue to work to do so! We want to get all those negative thought-habits out of our way! And during the process, we begin manifesting little successes while creating a life of positive thought-habits.

It's essential that you give yourself the time and patience to work through your list of doubts one by one until genuine conviction is found with your intention. Where you are is PERFECT! It's what makes you uniquely who you are. And as you work toward genuine conviction, your life will become more satisfying and you'll build up an arsenal of affirmations to share with others.

You'll know your intention is nearing conviction as you witness life start to manifest the intention in small and large ways! Pay close attention to the subtle feelings and impulses you get and follow them. As you practice doing so, leaps of faith become easier to make, and you can live a life of conviction!

Exercise

Take a moment now to repeat the intention you wrote down earlier. Do you hear any negative thoughts come up? If so, write them down and then write one affirmation that will focus your mind on the positive potential in that life situation. Recite the affirmation each morning for at least two weeks and then look yourself directly in the eyes in the mirror and repeat your intention again. This time, I bet you'll feel some conviction, knowing and becoming more certain of your belief in your intention.

Write any negative thoughts on the left and affirmations on the right:

_____   _____

_____   _____

_____   _____

_____   _____

_____   _____

Once you have absolute conviction in your intention, we can turn to the second principle of a CLEAR intention: Longing.

Longing

Once our intention has solid conviction to stand on, we can turn to the second principle, which is in having a genuine longing for that intention to be made manifest in our life.

It has to be something that we genuinely desire.

I think of longing as coming from our hearts rather than our heads. It isn't just something that sounds logical or rational, it's something we feel in our hearts. Intentions may have a rational and logical element to them, but the seed of the intention isn't based just on this; otherwise, when we're faced with difficulties, we would run the risk of logically and rationally dismantling our dreams.

A longing is something that we **hope** for. In fact, we hope beyond reason that the longing in our heart is to become realized. Hope is powerful stuff. Hope gives us the ability to move beyond challenges to attract necessary elements into our lives to make manifest our intention.

Ensure a genuine conviction first!

Just to be clear, we don't want to have a longing before conviction! Longing without conviction leads to neediness. If I desire something for my life, but I don't believe I can have it, I'm in the state of being needy: longing without a sense of hope.

If I long for an intimate relationship, but I don't believe I can find one, I have a desire that cannot be filled. This neediness will create disharmony in my life, leading potentially to physical as well as mental and emotional **dis**-ease. Therefore it's of the utmost importance that we test our intention for absolute conviction first. Once our conviction is sound, we can then move on to longing.

Healthy longing gives you a sense of purpose.

As we progress toward fulfilling our longing, we're filled with a sense of purpose in life. A genuine longing, coming from the heart, is a clue to what will bring joy, satisfaction, and fulfillment into our lives, and as we take the steps necessary to fill this longing, we move more and more toward a purpose-filled life.

Another way to state this is that we must acquire a certain amount of courage to pursue our intention. And that courage comes from hope. As we hope, which stretches beyond reason, that our longing is fulfilled, our life slowly begins to resemble the one we desire.

A craving or addiction is not a longing.

There are two times when a longing is not genuine: when it's a craving or an addiction. I imagine a scale where craving is at one end and addiction at the other. The best possible situation is one in which we are directly in the middle, far from the extremes. It's worth noting that there are times that an intention will oscillate from one extreme to the other while we are refining and defining it before manifesting it in our life.

A craving is an exciting idea
that is quickly abandoned.

Oftentimes, I think I have a genuine longing, but in fact, it's just a **craving**. A craving is a passing interest that temporarily pops up, sometimes incredibly fully formed and vivid and exciting, but shortly thereafter is dropped. It has no foundation. It's something I dream up one day and then forget about the next. It's the project I start one day and then delay finishing the next and the next until it gets forgotten.

It's easy to get carried away by the excitement and charge of the initial idea but then lose the drive to continue once the honeymoon buzz has passed. I think we all have had at least one time in which we were caught up in the excitement of the idea but let it drop soon afterward when the next new idea came along or something challenged it.

This is a natural part of discovering who we are, who we wish to be, where we wish to go in life. And, I would say, it's a healthy part of our evolution. It's a form of heart-based brainstorming, testing out different passions to see which one fits. The key is to learn from our cravings and to use them as a guide to find our genuine longings.

An addiction has
an unhealthy power over us.

Oftentimes, I think I have a genuine longing, but in fact it's an **addiction** over which I have little or no control. Addictions come in many forms, subtle and sometimes not so subtle, that manifest in every aspect of our lives: physical, emotional, and mental. We can have addictions to activities such as shopping or watching television. We can have addictions to emotional support from others. And an obvious addiction is when we have an unhealthy physical need for something like alcohol, drugs, or for me, chocolate chip cookies. (I can't trust myself around them!)

Life tests us to weed out
cravings and addictions!

The test for longing comes when our intention is tested! And our intentions will get tested! The universe hears us say, "My intention is . . ." and responds, "Oh yeah? What about now?" This helps purify our intentions and leads to manifesting our truest desires.

> *If my intention is "to take care of my body through exercising," the next morning something will come up that challenges my spending time exercising.*

> *If my intention is "to be loving to my partner," the next time we get together, something will happen to challenge my being loving.*

Knowing we'll be tested, it becomes almost funny when it happens. Celebrate the test as an opportunity to refine a desire to ensure the highest reality is made manifest.

A clear intention comes
with commitment and freedom!

A clear intention, from a healthy place of genuine longing, comes with the commitment and freedom to patiently allow things to change and evolve toward our desired reality.

If my intention is "to eat healthy," but I go out and gorge on a greasy dinner, I'm faced with the option of giving up on my intention, meaning it was just a passing interest, a craving. Or I could go crazy and mentally beat myself up, and then force myself to go on a fast for three days, which would indicate I have an unhealthy addiction to my intention. But if I remain committed and allow the freedom for my life to evolve naturally toward my intention, which often involves setbacks and plateaus, then I can be confident my intention is a genuine longing.

If my intention is "to think positive," how do I react to the next negative thought? If I give up on trying, it was probably just a craving. Or if I beat myself up, it's an addiction. But if I honor myself and patiently hope I'll think in more and more positive ways, then it's a genuine longing.

You'll know you have a genuine longing when you remain hopeful despite challenges!

Exercise

A test for longing is to imagine the intention NOT being realized the way you desire, whether in the time you wish or in the way you picture it. Do you still hope for it? Do you allow it to manifest in a way other than you imagined?

Write any thoughts or reasons to give up on the left and any harsh feelings on the right.

_____   _____

_____   _____

_____   _____

Now, write out a commitment to allowing the freedom for your intention to be fulfilled naturally.

_____

_____

_____

Once you have a genuine longing for your intention, we can turn to the third principle of a CLEAR intention: Embraced.

Embraced

A CLEAR intention is one we're willing to embrace being manifest, which means we're willing to allow it into our lives AND willing to do what's necessary to bring it into our lives.

Are we willing to receive AND surrender to pursuing?

It's easier to ask for things than to receive them! And it's far easier to say that we intend to do something than to actually go out and live that truth. The idea of an intention being embraced is in our asking ourselves if we're genuinely willing to receive it. And more importantly and perhaps more telling of whether we're willing to embrace our intention is the extent to which we're willing to surrender to the path we must take in order to receive it.

The saying "be careful what you wish for, because you just may get it" is at work here. Sometimes the thing we desire brings about more, or requires more from us, than we had bargained for.

If my intention is "to be an actor," but I'm unwilling to take a role that isn't the lead, unwilling to receive the fulfillment of my intention unless it's on my terms, or at least the way in which I fantasize about it manifesting, then I'm not genuinely willing to embrace it. What's more, taking the part that isn't the lead may be the path the universe has chosen to prepare me for the ultimate manifestation of my intention, but my unwillingness to surrender to the path sends a message to the universe that I'm not willing to genuinely embrace my intention.

If my intention is "to have a fulfilling career," but I am unwilling to put together a resume or go on interviews, or I just can't bring myself to say "good-bye" to my current colleagues and move on, then I'm not showing a willingness to surrender to the path necessary to manifest my intention. I'm not willing to embrace my intention.

Visualize what needs to shift!

The test for our willingness to embrace our intention is to visualize what needs to shift in our lives to bring that intention into reality AND to visualize how our lives will be shifted once we realize our intentions. If we're unable or unwilling to allow for this shift, or frightened by the possibilities of what the shift will result in, then we're not ready to embrace our intentions.

Exercise

Test your willingness to embrace your intention.

Take a moment now to visualize what needs to shift in your life and how your life would look once your intention is realized. Be honest about areas you're **hesitant to allow change in** (giving up sleeping in, giving up anonymity, giving up the freedom from responsibility) or **hesitant to be willing to do** (long workweeks, overtime, strict exercise/diet, financial requirements).

Write what needs to shift on the left and affirm your willingness to embrace this shift on the right.

_____   _____

_____   _____

_____   _____

_____   _____

Write what you'll have to do on the left and affirm your willingness to do these things on the right.

_____   _____

_____   _____

_____   _____

Once we feel a willingness to embrace our intentions, we can move on to the biggest piece of the puzzle in creating a CLEAR intention: Aligned.

Aligned

Our intention is aligned if it's free from nonintegrated thinking. Nonintegrated thinking is when our intentions conflict with other intentions and goals, or with deeply held, and sometimes unconscious, beliefs and values.

If I have an intention for something, but I have nonintegrated thinking, I'm setting myself up for frustration, as my inner conflict will sabotage my efforts to manifest my intention.

Align goals and intentions with a Feng Shui Life Map!

Start by eliminating nonintegrated thinking or conflicts between your intention and other intentions and goals.

For example, if I have a goal to live in a million-dollar house and I also have a goal of making a $60,000-a-year income, the two goals conflict. I couldn't afford a million-dollar home on a $50,000-a-year income. My nonintegrated thinking with these two goals will prevent my succeeding.

Eliminating nonintegrated thinking between our intentions and other goals and intentions is made possible as we create a Feng Shui Life Map. In chapter 5, we'll start creating our Feng Shui Life Map, and you'll begin by setting one intention and one goal in each of the Nine Life Areas. As you write out your intentions and goals you can more easily identify where there may be conflicts.

Moreover, this process allows us to see where we may have an imbalance in our lives, such as when we place more attention and energy in one Life Area, like career, over another, like relationships. Creating a written set of intentions and goals for all Nine Life Areas heals nonintegrated thinking between intentions and goals.

Self-awareness leads to alignment
with values and beliefs!

Aligning our intentions with our beliefs and values requires soul-searching awareness. This is because much of the nonintegrated thinking that comes as a result of conflicting values and beliefs stems from unconsciously held values and beliefs. These are the automatic thought-habits and conditioning that are so ingrained in our psyche we may not consciously recognize the conflict.

For example, if my intention is "to be wealthy," but I hold the unconscious, conflicting belief that rich people are self-centered snobs, I have nonintegrated thinking. I don't go around telling everyone that I think rich people are snobs, but the belief is still there and has a powerful effect on me. It prevents me from becoming wealthy, as I wouldn't want to think of myself as a snob.

More commonly, an unconsciously held conflict to wealth is the belief that there's a limited amount of resources and that if I have some, someone else has to do with less. Many of us were raised with this negative thought-habit and do not discover we operate from it until we come into contact with someone who's free from that belief. Our negative thought-habit becomes exposed and challenged. We then have to find a way to explain away the new evidence or shift our thinking.

The first step to eliminate nonintegrated thinking between our intentions and our values and beliefs is to stop and ask ourselves, "What value does this intention honor?" when we're setting an intention. Aligning intentions directly from the start with our values gives a solid foundation for our intentions.

Work with a teacher!

Discovering and eliminating all nonintegrated thinking takes time, patience, and a willingness to shift. Those who make this shift are the ones who are working with an objective and loving teacher. This teacher must truly be both objective and loving, offering critical feedback without judgment. It may not be a best friend or roommate, who may take our side or cushion the truth in niceties.

The test for our intentions being aligned comes with this objective feedback. Tell your intention to someone you trust and ask for his or her objective feedback. Ask someone who knows you thoroughly, understands your motivations and habits and can help guide you toward eliminating nonintegrated thinking altogether.

Inside out and outside in!

A Feng Shui Life Map approaches alignment from the inside out: creating a balanced set of intentions and goals for all Nine Life Areas first. Remember that intentions are stronger than any obstacle and will overcome any environmental obstacles and lead to our success.

And once the intentions are set with a Feng Shui Life Map, we can approach alignment from the outside in. Assessing one's environment through Feng Shui identifies how the elements of one's life are being reflected in one's environment, and then works to remove obstacles and create reflections that support one's intentions.

It's fun, it's powerful, and it's so easy to create Visual Affirmations to reflect our intentions, which leads us to the last principle of CLEAR Intention: Reflected!

Exercise

The test for alignment comes first from creating a balanced set of intentions for all Nine Life Areas (which we'll do in chapter 5), second, by identifying what value it honors, and third, by receiving feedback we from an objective and loving friend.

Identify and write out the value or belief that you hold that your intention honors:

_____

_____

_____

Email or call a friend you trust to be objective and loving and ask for his or her feedback on your intention. Write this feedback here:

_____

_____

_____

Once our intention is in alignment, let's set a Visual Affirmation of the intention by creating a reflection of it in our environment.

Reflected

The final principle in creating a CLEAR Intention is for it to be reflected throughout our environment. A clear intention needs to be reflected visually. This reminds us of our intention and reinforces the creation of new thought-habits to shift our thinking, which activates the Law of Attraction to begin attracting that new reality into our life.

Our environment must reflect our intention!

If my intention is "to eat healthy," but when I go into my kitchen all I find is junk food, then my intention is going to be weighed down, blocked, or may get lost and abandoned.

If I have a strong intention to eat healthy, then I'll go out and find healthy food, and the obstacles will be overcome. But if I wish to set a CLEAR Intention, I'm going to get rid of the obstacles and create a visual affirmation of my intention.

A completed Feng Shui Life Map is not only a complete Visual Affirmation, it's also a guide to assess reflections in our environment. Lay the Map over the floor plan and go into each area and see how your intentions and goals are being reflected. You can create an environment that's supportive.

It's a two-step process:
Create space and create a Reflection.

Creating a supportive environment is a two-step process: the first step is in creating space for new energies to flow into and around; the second step is in creating a reflection of our intention that directs those new energies toward a particular and desired reality!

> *For example, one client wanted a new career. We went to his career area, which was his kitchen, and noted all counter space was packed with gadgets and dishes and stacks of papers. The universe couldn't bring him a new career, as he didn't have any space for it! Even if he wanted to cook, he'd have to first clear some counter space to do that.*
>
> *So our first step was to create space. We put away the dishes and mail and gave away some of the unused appliances he'd collected and. There was now space for the universe to bring in new energies.*

Next, we created a reflection of his intention to direct the new energies. In his case, we brought in a new breadbox with the intention of it representing a new income, new bread from a new career.

Unused, unloved, unfinished = energy depletion.

Anything that is unused, unloved, or unfinished creates disharmony and causes stress in our lives by distracting our attention and gobbling up the energy we could be using to deal with other things.

Address the emotional attachment first!

Addressing these items can be like therapy, as they often carry some emotional energy. We're required to make a decision, finish something we've been avoiding or discard something that we haven't let go of yet.

To deal with the emotional attachment, I have a three-step solution:

First, have in mind a clear idea of what it is that you DO wish to manifest in your life. Create a clear image of this reality. The clearer the image we hold, the more powerful the motivation to start clearing.

Second, observe yourself objectively. View yourself as if watching a movie while you're clearing clutter, and when emotions pop up, say, "oh, look, that person is experiencing emotions attached to that object!" And then take command of the scene and remind yourself of what it is you're clearing space for in your life and move on!

Third, clear in very tiny steps. It's obvious where the clutter has collected in our environment, but that obvious spot is probably not the best place to start! Start someplace easy, I mean, really, really easy! One tiny spot cleared will give you more energy, and these little cleared spots add up so that the big clutter spot (the garage or the desk or the closet) will be easier because you'll have the energy for it!

Once an area is clear, have a ceremony!

The second step in this process is to create a Reflection. Whenever an area becomes clear of clutter, no matter how small or how great, have a celebration and ceremony to welcome in new energies. Then create Visual Affirmations of new realities in your life. The process becomes so fun it's addictive. Find one token object that affirms your intentions and place it in the clutter-free space as a reflection of that intention. This visual reminder will shift thought-habits, activate the Law of Attraction, and begin making manifest your dreams!

The best Reflection is a Feng Shui Life Map — it's balanced and complete, and because it's visual it evokes powerful shifts in your life!

Exercise

Let today be the day that you transform some small spot of clutter in your life to create a visual reflection of your intention:

1. Place the Bagua over your floor plan and identify the area of your home that correlates to the Life Area in which you set an intention at the beginning of this chapter.

2. Go to that area and clear some space for the new energy to come in. If it's already clutter-free, GREAT!

3. Next, come up with one small token that'll visually remind you of your intention and can be placed in this area. Maybe it'll be a vase with flowers, a candle, a note, a picture, a charm from a bracelet, or whatever inspires you.

4. Smile, knowing your intention is being made manifest!

Extra credit! Clearing clutter exercises

Bedroom

1. Clear items out from under the bed. If you've invested in an expensive under-the-bed storage system, or your space requires you to use this area for storage, then be extremely vigilant to keep the area organized and free from excess and unused items.

2. Next, tackle the closet — ah, the place of forgotten items! For many people, this may take several passes, and that's OK! You can also make a game out of it, inviting your best friend over for a fashion show where you can get the thumbs-up or thumbs-down to discard unnecessary items.

Kitchen

1. Start by clearing out the fridge! Give the compost a workout, discarding any expired items or foods you know you'll no longer use. And give the fridge a good wash. Think of it as if you were cleaning out all your insides and getting rid of any stuck energies, disease, and disharmony in your body!

2. Next, clean the stovetop. The stove's burners represent avenues of abundance coming into our lives. One Feng Shui trick I like to share is to use a different burner each time you use the stove. We get in the habit of using the same burner over and over, but by using different ones each time, you're letting the universe know that you wish to be open to receiving abundance from four different avenues (or six or eight or however many).

3. Last, clear out the drawers and cupboards. Get rid of broken or unused items. Again, think of each broken bowl you toss out as a cavity that was growing in your mouth. You're much better off without it!

Entryway

1. Remove any recycling bins, trash, or unused flowerpots from the entrance.

2. Clutter-free the entryway closet and keep only seasonal items in there.

3. If you have a drop table inside the door, be sure that its neat and not piled up with the mail and other items awaiting attention. A nice basket on the table could hold these items and keep the table neat.

Intention exercise - Review

Rewrite the intention you wrote at the beginning of this chapter, applying all the principles of CLEAR as you rewrite it.

_____

_____

_____

_____

CLEAR Intention worksheet

Use this worksheet with each new intention to create a CLEAR Intention!

CONVICTION Do you genuinely believe in it? Write any doubts that come up when you speak your intention aloud on the left, and then write affirmations to create new thought-habits and short-circuit those doubts on the right.

_____   _____

_____   _____

_____   _____

LONGING Do you genuinely desire this intention in your life? Imagine your intention NOT being made manifest in the manner you desire, and then write any thoughts/reasons/feeling of wanting to give up on the left and any intense feelings of "having to do it" on the right.

_____   _____

_____   _____

_____   _____

Now, write a commitment to patiently allow the freedom for your intention to be fulfilled naturally.

_____

_____

_____

_____

EMBRACED Are you willing to receive this new reality, and are you willing to surrender to the path necessary to manifest it in your life? Write out what needs to shift in your life on the left and an affirmation to affirm your willingness to allow it on the right.

_____   _____

_____   _____

_____   _____

ALIGNED Is your intention in line with your values? Write out what value your intention honors. Tell your intention to a friend and ask for feedback on any conflicts he or she sees it may have.

_____

_____

_____

_____

_____

REFLECTED Is your intention reflected in your environment? Write down one token visual symbol you can create and place in your home to represent your intention.

_____

_____

_____

CLEAR Intention worksheet

Use this worksheet with each new intention to create a CLEAR Intention!

CONVICTION Do you genuinely believe in it? Write any doubts that come up when you speak your intention aloud on the left, and then write affirmations to create new thought-habits and short-circuit those doubts on the right.

_____   _____

_____   _____

_____   _____

LONGING Do you genuinely desire this intention in your life? Imagine your intention NOT being made manifest in the manner you desire, and then write any thoughts/reasons/feeling of wanting to give up on the left and any intense feelings of "having to do it" on the right.

_____   _____

_____   _____

_____   _____

Now, write a commitment to patiently allow the freedom for your intention to be fulfilled naturally.

_____

_____

_____

_____

EMBRACED Are you willing to receive this new reality, and are you willing to surrender to the path necessary to manifest it in your life? Write out what needs to shift in your life on the left and an affirmation to affirm your willingness to allow it on the right.

_____   _____

_____   _____

_____   _____

ALIGNED Is your intention in line with your values? Write out what value your intention honors. Tell your intention to a friend and ask for feedback on any conflicts he or she sees it may have.

_____

_____

_____

_____

_____

REFLECTED Is your intention reflected in your environment? Write down one token visual symbol you can create and place in your home to represent your intention.

_____

_____

_____

Chapter 3

SMART Goals

CLEAR Intentions lead to SMART Goals! Now that you're empowered to create CLEAR Intentions, this chapter provides the tools for constructing goals that will successfully affirm CLEAR Intentions. The acronym SMART, which has been tweaked somewhat from its common usage, provides the steps to creating a goal that will ensure continued motivation and success.

Setting Goals based on your Intention

Goals focus on a particular future reality. Having a goal is essential to moving us forward in life, and the benefits of having goals are enormous. But the essential first step to setting any goal is to begin with an awareness of the intention that's driving it. And for this reason, I suggest that the previous chapter on Intentions be read and understood completely before beginning this chapter on Goals.

To review Intentions and Goals:

- A Goal is the WHAT and an Intention is the WHY. What is it that we wish to accomplish (goal), and why is it that we wish to accomplish it (intention)?

- Intentions provide us direction through the ever-changing flow of life so that if a goal is blocked, delayed, abandoned, or changed in some way, our Intention will help keep us moving in our desired direction.

- The easiest way to tell the difference between goals and intentions is to ask if the expressed desire has an outcome. If it does, it's a goal. Intentions do not have end points, goals do.

- The desire to give up comes only if we're unaware of our intentions or do not have a CLEAR Intention. Awareness of our intentions will lead us to find new goals in the face of challenges.

In this chapter, we'll be discussing the principles of setting SMART Goals. SMART is an acronym, and my use of SMART is particular to setting goals after a CLEAR Intention has been laid as the foundation.

As with the acronym CLEAR, it's worth the time to apply all of the principles of the SMART acronym to each of our goals in order to ensure the best possibility of success.

Goal exercise

Let's begin by coming up with one goal based on the intention you worked on in the last chapter. What's one future reality you wish to see manifest based on the intention you set?

Write your goal here:

_____

_____

_____

_____

_____

Now, let's go through the principles of SMART and see how we can ensure your goal is as smart as possible.

Specific

The first step to creating a SMART Goal is to make certain that it emphasizes what it is that we desire to happen in clear, certain detail. "Specific" means that the wording is pointing our energies directly ahead, like a laser beam locked on a specific target. It's moving us forward in a straight line.

No confusion! No compromise! No ambiguity!

The idea is to define our goal in the most specific terms possible so that there's no doubt as to where EXACTLY we are heading. And the way to do this is to include as many specific details as possible.

Rather than make it a goal to live in a new house, make it a goal to live in a 4-bedroom, 3-bath modern home with a rooftop deck, lush wooded surroundings, and a view of the setting sun.

The more specific the information I send out into the universe, the greater the likelihood that it'll respond with exactly what it is that I desire. The more general I am, the more general the universe responds.

Success you can witness!

If we don't know what it is that we're aiming for, we won't know when we achieve it. Being specific allows us to recognize when our goals are being made manifest. Broad, general goals provide direction and lead to success, but the success is not as easily noticed. And being able to notice our goals being manifest gives us encouragement and motivation to strive for more, set new goals, and achieve more in life.

Drill down to the specifics!

Many times our not being able to be specific is due to our thinking too far into the future for us to see it clearly. Start with the short-term, with what you do know, and set specific goals for that reality. As those realities become manifest, the future will become more clear as well.

Not everyone has a clear idea of where he or she wishes to be in ten years, and this is one reason to practice Feng Shui Life Mapping on the Short-Term Path. On the Short-Term Path, we set goals that can be achieved in two weeks. Every two weeks, we can review our accomplishments and refine our goals.

The universe is NOT
without a sense of humor!

Another reason I suggest beginning on the Short-Term Path is that it gives us the opportunity to see just how the Law of Attraction works. Remember that the Law of Attraction is indiscriminate; it doesn't differentiate between what we desire and what we do not, it merely brings in whatever it is that we focus our attention on.

Many times I have witnessed someone placing a visual affirmation in his or her space or a picture of something on their Feng Shui Life Map and attracting that exact thing into their lives. And once this happens, the person realizes he or she wasn't specific enough.

> *One of my clients created a Vision Board that had the picture of a married man in her Love & Partnership Area. She got exactly what she asked for, a married man! She cut that image out and replaced it with a man proposing marriage instead.*

Be open to becoming specific!

Sometimes we may not have a complete picture of what it is that we desire. Here, we can start with the goal of moving toward defining that desire in detail. If this is where you feel you are, celebrate the infinite possibilities that are before you and set a goal to become more clear.

Describe your goal to a friend.

The test for a goal being specific is in telling it to a friend and asking what he or she imagines. If we're specific with clear and certain details, they'll get exactly the same image we have in our heads.

If my goal is to get a new car, I can tell my friend I wish to get a new car and ask what image he or she has. If it's the image of a sedan, but I'm thinking more of an SUV, I need to get more specific! I can work with my friend to get specific, defining my goal as getting a brand-new, four-door, red, hybrid SUV with black leather interior and an oversized sunroof.

Exercise

Review the goal you wrote at the beginning of this chapter. Write in more details for it in order to create the most specific goal possible.

Details:

_____   _____

_____   _____

_____   _____

Tell your goal to a friend and ask him or her to describe what end result they get.

_____

_____

_____

_____

_____

Once our goal is specific, we can then make sure it's Measurable.

Measurable

A SMART goal is quantifiable. "Measurable" means that the results can be tracked and calculated as we progress toward the finish line. Measurable is a key area in which we need to be specific.

"I will read more" is not measurable. We may be able to say we read more, but as it's so loosely defined, we're left open to nonobjective measures to determine if we're moving in the right direction. Stating that same goal as "I'll read three books of one hundred pages each" will give us a measurable goal.

Measuring success creates motivation for more success!

When we choose a goal with measurable results, we can see the changes as they occur and gain encouragement. We can pat ourselves on the back for what we've accomplished and feel so invigorated from this little pat that we get motivated to keep going, reaching for the goal's completion.

More importantly, if the goal isn't measurable, we won't know when we've completed it, when we can start the celebration!!!

Measure even the nonquantifiable goals!

Many goals may seem impossible to measure because they relate to our quality of life. These are the goals of being happier or having a better relationship or feeling better. With quality goals, measurability depends on our being specific!

Break the goal down to create a more specific picture of what makes that quality of life better. A better relationship may be defined as "having one meaningful conversation each week." Being happier may be defined as "rating my day as a 6 or higher on a scale of 1 to 10."

Ask yourself, "What defines this 'quality' for me?" And let that become the measuring stick.

Take note of your progress!

To improve your success, start the habit of charting your progress! Write your goal at the top of a page, and each day of the week, make a notation on the progress. This practice will also give you a way to stay on top of changes that need to be made to the goal as life flows along its course. You win when you're flexible and remain committed to a goal even when it needs to be adjusted!

Exercise

Take a look at your goal, is it measurable? Can you clearly determine when you've accomplished it? What's more, will you be able to see if you're heading in the direction of your goal?

Write some measurements for your goal, some "goal posts" you anticipate crossing as you pursue your goal.

_____

_____

_____

_____

_____

Once we have a Specific and Measurable goal, we can go on to a big principle: Ambitious!

Ambitious

A SMART goal is ambitious!!! By "ambitious," I mean it's **excitingly challenging**! "Exciting," in that it gets us motivated, and "challenging," in that it pushes us beyond our known boundaries.

Goals need to stretch us!

A SMART goal is set at that point beyond our comfort zone but before our breaking point.

A goal that aims too low will send a message to my unconscious that I'm not capable. It's a blow to my confidence and an insult to my abilities. More importantly, such a goal will drain my motivation to work toward it. Not only does it appear so simple that I think I can do it easily and I don't really need to focus any attention on it now, but I don't feel I'll really be accomplishing anything by doing it so I won't even try.

The anticipation of success
fosters motivation!

Just as damaging to our motivation as aiming too low, aiming too high will send a message to my unconscious that it just isn't possible and thus not worth trying. I may have hopeful idealism, but the knowledge that it's too much for me leads my subconscious to find ways to avoid action or give a genuine effort.

In keeping goals ambitious and not too high, ensure it's humanly possible. For example, if I wish to lose weight and make it my goal to lose twenty pounds in one week. That isn't humanly possible — at least not safely. A more humanly possible and safe goal would be to lose two pounds in one week, and once I reach that goal, aim to lose another two pounds the following week.

One test for the ambitiousness of a goal is to write out the steps necessary to accomplishing it as a to-do list. Detailing the stages will help point out any gaps we have in getting from A to B.

What would your parents say?

Determining if your goal is ambitious is a very personal quest. But one test I like to give is to imagine what your parents would say were you to tell them your goal. Most parents have the idea of our being more capable than we believe ourselves to be, and that's just the sort of ambition we need to aim for to create big shifts in our lives!

Exercise

Test your goal's Ambitiousness!!!

What steps do you foresee in the process toward accomplishing your goal?

_____

_____

What would your parents say if you told them your goal?

_____

_____

What would make your goal more ambitious?

_____

_____

What would make your goal more realistic?

_____

_____

Once our Goal is ambitious, we can move on to making sure it's Reaffirming!

Reaffirming

A SMART goal is Reaffirming! It's

- stated in the positive
- stated in the present tense
- accompanied by Affirmations

Reaffirming addresses the language we use to verbalize our goal. How we send the message out to the universe determines much of how the universe responds.

Get a positive response!

The first step in creating a Reaffirming goal is to ensure it's stated in the positive. Stating the goal in the positive means that it expresses what we wish to do, rather than what we wish to stop doing or cease having as a part of our life.

If my goal is to stop eating junk food, I can state it in the positive by saying, "My goal is to choose foods that are good for my body." Or perhaps I'd say, "My goal is to choose a healthy snack."

When we state the goal in the negative, we're setting up a battle, a war! We're giving energy to that thing we wish to cease because we're actively pushing against it. If we stop pushing, it ceases to exist! There are a number of books on the philosophy of nonresistance. Basically, when we state our goal in the positive, we're directing the universe to respond positively to us.

Use active language!

A Reaffirming goal is stated in the present tense, meaning we watch for phrases like "going to," which puts things off to some future point. If my goal is "I'm going to read that book," I've created a goal that leaves me in the state of being "about to do it," but never quite getting to it!

"Trying to" is another delaying phrase in our society. It's so commonly used, it's practically unconscious script. Count how many times you hear someone say, "trying to" in one day. It's amazing! "Trying to" sets us out on the right course, but it lacks direct action and leaves us always in the state of trying but not doing.

And a word I personally watch for is "want." The word "want" comes from the Latin word meaning "to be deficient" and means "to be lacking."

When we say, "I want a cookie," what we're actually saying is "I'm lacking a cookie." When "want" pops up, I substitute the words "desire" or "wish."

The best way to keep our goal stated in a Reaffirming manner is to start with "My goal is to . . ." For example, "My goal is to eat a healthy meal today" or "My goal is to buy a new red sports car." From that foundation, natural grammar will lead to supportive and active language.

Affirmations build support!

The final key to Reaffirming is for the goal to be accompanied by affirmations. Affirmations short-circuit any doubts of our goal being fulfilled by creating new thought-habits to reinforce our ability to manifest the goal.

Affirmations are different than goals in that they state the goal as though it's happening now or already happened. A goal starts with "My goal is . . ." and an affirmation starts with "I now (have/am/am doing) . . ." Affirmations are essential to building a solid foundation to manifesting our desires.

If my goal is to exercise four times a week, I can have an affirmation that states, "I'm exercising four times a week." If my goal is to complete my certification course, I can have an affirmation that states, "I now have my certification." This affirmation creates a visual image of my goal being completed, thus solidifying my conviction in achieving it.

Exercise

Test the Reaffirming language of your goal:

Is your goal stated in the positive? If not, reword it in the positive.

_____

_____

Is your goal stated in the present tense? Reword your goal starting with the phrase "My goal is to . . ." and see how it sounds and feels.

_____

_____

Write at least one affirmation to accompany your goal.

_____

_____

And with our Goal being Reaffirming, we can move on to the last SMART principle: Timely!

Timely

A SMART Goal has a deadline, an end point: next week, three months, by the end of the year, or whatever future point feels right.

Deadlines foster motivation!

Putting an end point on a goal gives a clear target to works toward. If I don't set a deadline, I'm less likely to commit to doing it because I get the sense I can start any time. I'm giving myself an open window to start whenever I feel like, as I don't have a clear idea of when I wish to finish.

Moreover, without a deadline, there's no sense of urgency to start now. We all work best under a healthy amount of pressure. If there's no pressure, we're likely to lack motivation. If there's too much, we may give up before trying. Just as our goal itself needs to be Ambitious, our deadline needs to be ambitious as well, stretching us slightly but not breaking us.

Balance is the key to Feng Shui.

It's also important to have a balance between short-term and long-term goals.

If I have five long-term goals that all take two years to achieve, then that means for two years I'll be pressing toward my goals without ever having the satisfaction of accomplishing something. Some have the willpower to maintain such discipline. Personally, I know that I don't. Short-term goals balance out long-term goals.

However, if I have only short-term goals and no long-term goals, I won't have a clear focus for the future. It's great to frequently be achieving something, but why am I achieving it? Without long-term goals all I'll have is a bunch of passing successes that, in the long run, don't add up to much.

Go with the FLOW!

Having a Timely goal means having a deadline, but — and this is a BIG but! — a SMART goal is able to go with the flow. Life unfolds in ways we don't always imagine. Sometimes we realize we have to revise a goal as circumstances change. When this happens, drop any feelings of failure and instead consider it a victory to have recognized the need to adjust, and then transform the goal to more appropriate terms.

Exercise

Test your goal for being Timely.

Does the goal have a deadline? Is the deadline ambitious and still realistic? Write in a few alternative times and see which feels best.

_____

_____

_____

Write up a plan B if the goal doesn't unfold the way you imagine it!

_____

_____

_____

Congratulations! With your Goal being Timely, you now have a SMART Goal! You're heading for success!

Goal exercise - Review

Rewrite the Goal you wrote at the beginning of this chapter, applying all the principles of SMART as you rewrite it.

_____

_____

_____

_____

When we create a SMART Goal from a CLEAR Intention, we ensure our manifesting that reality in our lives.

Having learned the principles of CLEAR and SMART, you're now ready to create a balanced and complete set of intentions and goals for all Nine Life Areas of the Feng Shui Bagua as the start of your Feng Shui Life Map.

Keep in mind that applying all the principles of CLEAR and SMART takes time, but it's time well spent!

SMART Goal worksheet

Use this worksheet with each new goal to ensure it's a SMART Goal!

SPECIFIC Write in as much detail as possible for your goal.

_____   _____

_____   _____

_____   _____

Tell your goal to a friend and ask him or her to describe what end result they imagine.

_____

_____

_____

MEASURABLE Is your goal measurable? Write some measurements for your goal, some "goal posts" you anticipate crossing in the pursuit of your goal.

_____

_____

_____

AMBITIOUS What would your parents say if you told them your goal?

_____

_____

REAFFIRMING Is your goal stated in the positive? If not, can you reword it to be in the positive?

_____

_____

Is your goal stated in the present tense? Reword your goal starting with the phrase "My goal is to . . ." and see how it sounds and feels.

_____

_____

Write at least one affirmation to accompany your goal.

_____

_____

TIMELY Test your goal for being Timely. Does the goal have a deadline? Is the deadline ambitious and still realistic? Write in a few alternative times and see which feels best, and write up a plan B in case the goal doesn't unfold the way you imagine it.

_____

_____

SMART Goal worksheet

Use this worksheet with each new goal to ensure it's a SMART Goal!

SPECIFIC Write in as much detail as possible for your goal.

_____ _____

_____ _____

_____ _____

Tell your goal to a friend and ask him or her to describe what end result they imagine.

_____

_____

_____

MEASURABLE Is your goal measurable? Write some measurements for your goal, some "goal posts" you anticipate crossing in the pursuit of your goal.

_____

_____

_____

AMBITIOUS What would your parents say if you told them your goal?

_____

_____

REAFFIRMING Is your goal stated in the positive? If not, can you reword it to be in the positive?

_____

_____

Is your goal stated in the present tense? Reword your goal starting with the phrase "My goal is to . . ." and see how it sounds and feels.

_____

_____

Write at least one affirmation to accompany your goal.

_____

_____

TIMELY Test your goal for being Timely. Does the goal have a deadline? Is the deadline ambitious and still realistic? Write in a few alternative times and see which feels best, and write up a plan B in case the goal doesn't unfold the way you imagine it.

_____

_____

PART III

Feng Shui & Vision Boarding

Let go!
Let it flow!

CHAPTER 4

The Feng Shui
Secret Formula

This chapter begins to explore the vast world of Feng Shui, starting with the Feng Shui Bagua's Nine Life Areas. Approaching this study using the numerical order of the Bagua becomes a guide to understanding the flow of energy through our life, what I call the "Feng Shui Secret Formula to Life." Once we've traveled through all Nine Life Areas, we'll see how the Bagua can be applied to Feng Shui Life Mapping and discuss a few of the key principles of Feng Shui, which are necessary to this practice.

The Feng Shui Secret Formula to Life

The Feng Shui Secret Formula to Life takes a look at how energy flows through our life, following the numerical order of the Feng Shui Bagua.

The Feng Shui Bagua

The Feng Shui Bagua is an octagon-shaped map that depicts the locations of the Nine Life Areas. The eight sides and the center give us nine quadrants with each assigned to one Life Area. However, the Bagua is more commonly depicted in Western society with the octagon stretched into a square shape, with a tic-tac-toe in the middle to give us the Nine Life Areas. The picture below shows both the octagon shape and its being pulled out into a square, with the additional tic-tac-toe lines as they would look.

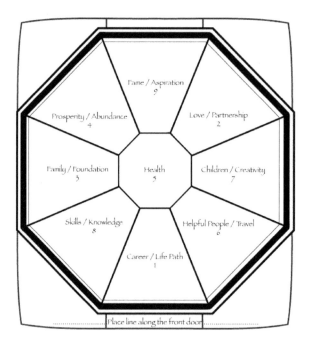

The Bagua is a guide to how energy flows through our life and, reflectively, through our environment. Understanding this flow empowers us to augment the flow of energy toward manifesting our dream life.

The Magic Square

Each Life Area of the Feng Shui Bagua has a number associated with it. Following energy along this numerical order gives us the Feng Shui Secret Formula to Life.

As energy flows through the Nine Life Areas along the numerical order of the Feng Shui Bagua, our ability to receive and use it ensures a fulfilling life.

This numerical order forms what's called a Magic Square. It's called so because the numbers can be added across, down, or diagonal and will always total fifteen.

4	9	2	= 15
3	5	7	= 15
8	1	6	= 15
=	=	=	=
15	15	15	15

Pure, raw energy begins its path through our lives entering Life Area 1: Career & Life Path. As the energy flows from one Life Area to the next, how we incorporate and use that energy will determine how the energy continues to flow to our other Life Areas.

Energy that flows freely enables us to harmonize all the Life Areas to create a balanced life and thereby support our intentions to make manifest our goals. With free-flowing energy, we can properly align ourselves and more importantly prepare ourselves for a successful and harmonious life.

Introducing the Nine Life Areas

To introduce the Nine Life Areas and how they flow, let's first take a look at the key concept and key action for each.

**The key action manifests
the key concept.**

As we practice the key action of each quadrant, we are empowered to begin realizing the full potential of that Life Area, the key concept. This happens gradually. Some actions may seem easier than others at the start, and they are! The fact is that each new energy flow in our lives will bring with it new opportunities to perfect our practice of the key actions.

As we now go through the Nine Life Areas briefly here, consider how the energy flows in that particular aspect of your life.

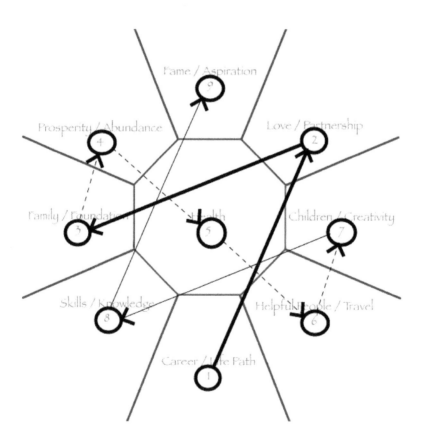

Life Area 1   **Career & Life Path**

Key Concept   Bliss

Key Action   Follow

Energy begins its flow through our life in the first quadrant, representing our Career & Life Path. This is where the universal energy connects with our individual soul and brings to life our soul's purpose. The key concept here is bliss, as in "follow your bliss." For as we take the key action of following our bliss, life slowly adjusts, and shifts, and begins to resemble more and more of a purpose-filled and satisfying life.

Life Area 2:   **Love & Partnership**

Key Concept   Openheartedness

Key Action   Trust

The energy moves from the first quadrant to the second, representing Love & Partnership. Here the energy connects with our hearts and enables us to receive and give unconditionally. The key concept here is openheartedness, for as we're able to open our hearts, energy can move freely in and out of our lives to create the best possible realities. The key action here is trust. As we're able to trust, we're able to open our hearts. This begins as we first trust in ourselves, and once that trust is solid, we can then trust in the universe and in others.

Life Area 3   **Family & Foundation**

Key Concept   Authenticity

Key Action   Accept

The energy moves to the fourth quadrant, representing Family & Foundation. Here the energy connects with the foundational set of values and beliefs we've developed as influenced by our familial relationships, both blood and surrogate. The key concept here is authenticity, as in being authentic about who we are. The key action here is to accept. Being authentic starts as we accept ourselves for who we really are, allowing energy to flow unimpeded by superficiality or falsehoods.

Life Area 4   **Prosperity & Abundance**

Key Concept   Gratitude

Key Action   Giving

The energy moves into the fourth quadrant representing Prosperity &
Abundance. The key concept here is gratitude, for abundance works on
the principle of gratitude. As we show gratitude for something, we
magnetically attract more of it into our life. Gratitude is best affirmed by
taking the key action of giving. This, too, begins as we generously give to
ourselves all that we need and desire, and continues to our being
generous toward others.

Life Area 5   **Health**

Key Concept   Vitality

Key Action   Support

The energy moves into the fifth quadrant, representing Health. This
represents both our physical and our emotional health. Just as what we
eat has the power to heal or to harm, how we digest the energies of life
can lead to strength and vigor or gas and heartburn. The key concept
here is vitality, for as we're able to gratefully receive the flow of energy,
our physical and emotional health is vitalized. The key action here is
support, as in our taking the necessary steps to ensure we're supported.
And from this supported place, we're then able to be of support to others.

Life Area 6   **Helpful People & Travel**

Key Concept   Synchronicity

Key Action   Surrender

The energy travels into the sixth quadrant, representing Helpful People &
Travel. As we travel out into the world, we meet others who recognize it
as their destiny to assist us along in our paths. The key concept here is
synchronicity, for as we allow the energy to flow smoothly we find we are
always in the right place at the right time, encountering just the right
person. This involves taking the key action of surrender. And by
"surrender," I mean both surrendering to our intuition and surrendering to
the way life unfolds.

Life Area 7   **Children & Creativity**

Key Concept   Limitless

Key Action   Express

The energy moves into our seventh quadrant, representing Children & Creativity. Here the universal energy is preparing to create something new, open a new door, and spawn new creations. The key concept here is limitless, for the possibilities of this infinite universe are truly as limitless as the imagination of a child. And the key action is express, for we're given the opportunity and the directive to express how the energies creatively inspire us.

Life Area 8   **Skills & Knowledge**

Key Concept   Cultivation

Key Action   Freedom

The energy moves into the eighth quadrant, representing Skills & Knowledge. The key concept here is cultivation, for the energies are ready to be reviewed, understood, and, from a grounded place, built on and expanded. The key action here is freedom, as in giving ourselves the freedom to decide to let go of experiences and choose new and different paths for ourselves. And as we allow ourselves this freedom, we're able to allow such freedom to others.

Life Area 9   **Fame & Aspiration**

Key Concept   Projection

Key Action   Promise

The energy moves into the ninth and final quadrant, representing Fame & Aspiration. The key concept here is projection, as we're projecting ourselves in how we wish to be been seen and known. This projection starts with the key action of promise, for as we make a promise, first to ourselves and then to others, we're showing a willingness to be held accountable for the reputation to which we aspire to having.

The Feng Shui Secret Formula to Life summarized

Quadrant	Key Concept	Key Action
Career & Life	Bliss	Follow
Love & Partnership	Openheartedness	Trust
Family & Foundation	Authenticity	Accept
Prosperity & Abundance	Gratitude	Giving
Health	Vitality	Support
Helpful People & Travel	Synchronicity	Surrender
Children & Creativity	Limitless	Express
Skills & Knowledge	Cultivation	Freedom
Fame & Aspiration	Projection	Promise

The Feng Shui Secret Formula to Life summarized

- Energy starts in our **Career & Life Path**, sparking to life our soul's purpose.

- It then flows to **Love & Partnership**, connecting with our open hearts to allow for unconditional giving and receiving.

- It then flows to **Family & Foundation**, and as we're true to ourselves, we're able to decide if the energy reflects our true nature or not. Given the auspicious chance that it is,

- It then flows to **Prosperity & Abundance**, where our gratitude magnetically draws more of it to us,

- Feeding vitality into our physical and emotional **Health**, and from that supported place,

- Sends us, **Traveling** out into the world to find **Helpful People**, who'll recognize it as their destiny to assist us. And perhaps some will also join us as . . .

- It flows to **Children & Creativity** where we begin new projects, with limitless new expressions.

- It then flows to **Skills & Knowledge**, where we can reflect on our path and, from this grounded place, determine where it is that we wish to go.

- And finally, it flows to **Fame & Aspiration**, launching us, like a shooting star, streaking across the heavens, projecting our light out into the universe to become famous for that which we aspire to be known.

Feng Shui Life Mapping concepts

To allow the energy to flow through our lives smoothly and harmoniously, Feng Shui Life Mapping incorporates several key Feng Shui concepts.

Feng Shui Acupuncture

Blocks at any point along the flow of energy through the Nine Life Areas cause the energy to become weighed down, sticky, and confused. This creates disharmony throughout all of our lives.

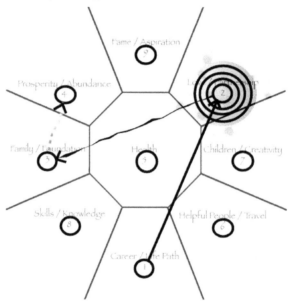

I liken this block along the flow of energy through the Bagua to blocks along energy meridians in the body. In the practice of acupuncture, we seek to discover these places and use tools to allow the energy to begin flowing again. In the same way, Feng Shui helps us discover where these blocks are and helps us correct both our environment and our mental and emotional makeup to get the energy flowing harmoniously again.

For more information on removing blocks, review the principle of Reflection, discussed as part of creating a CLEAR Intention in chapter 2. A Reflection is a simple two-step process of clearing space and creating a Visual Affirmation to enhance the harmonious flow of energy in our lives.

The importance of balance

A key principle of Feng Shui is creating balance. Ideally, we need to create balance in every aspect of our lives. This means keeping a balance between the yin and the yang of life, the positive and negative, the dark and the light, the expansive and the retracting, and so on. But moreover, keeping balance between the different Life Areas.

You can imagine what happens to the person who focuses all of his or her energies on the Prosperity & Abundance section. They may indeed find great wealth, but the opposite quadrant, the Travel & Helpful People Life Areas, is thrown off. These are the people who have money, but don't have anyone they can trust in their life, believing that everyone is after their money!

Or you can imagine what happens to the person who focuses all of his or her energies on the Love & Partnership Life Area. By doing so, the Skills & Knowledge quadrant is thrown off. These are the people who are constantly going out on dates and even having relationships, but because the Skills & Knowledge Life Area is not balanced with it, they aren't learning from their mistakes and will keep dating the same type of wrong person.

Or imagine the people who put all their energy in the Career & Life Path without creating balance with the Fame & Aspiration quadrant. They may rise to the top of the corporate ladder, but their reputation will be of a cutthroat, heartless, cold businessperson.

Balance is the key!

A Feng Shui trick I like to encourage is that whenever someone wants to effect a change in one Life Area, focus equally on that area and the opposite quadrant. In this way, a balance of intention and energy is put forth to create a solid foundation for the new reality to take hold!

Layer Feng Shui

We lay the Bagua over a space by aligning the bottom line with the entry area of the space. A common question is if we can lay the Bagua over an entire space, each room, or even smaller areas. It's a GREAT question! The answer is that the Bagua can be laid over each successive layer of your space, what I call Layer Feng Shui.

First, lay the Bagua over the entire **lot**, including the garden, the sidewalk, the driveway, and so forth. Then, lay the Bagua over the entire **floor**

plan of the building to include the kitchen, bedrooms, and so forth. And then use the Bagua for each individual **room**.

Intentions can then be amplified threefold by creating one Visual Affirmation at each layer — placing a new plant in your garden in the Love & Partnership, then placing a small statue or artwork in the Love & Partnership area of your house, which may be your kitchen, and finally placing a candle or item in the Love & Partnership area of each individual room.

You can even Feng Shui your desk, placing the Bagua on the desktop and adjusting items with intention in each area of the desktop!

This will quickly accelerate your manifesting the reality you desire.

Color associations of the quadrants

Obviously, there's a great deal more to Feng Shui! During a Feng Shui consultation, a professional would correlate each Life Area with its associated element (fire, water, metal, earth, wood), including their constructive and destructive cycles, and also incorporate several other associations each Life Area quadrant has: body part, time of day, season, shape . . . and so forth.

For the purpose of creating a Feng Shui Life Map, we're going to start with one key association, and that's the **COLOR** associated with each area. I share this because you may find it useful to find specific colors to go in each area as you design your Vision Board. Or you may choose to use markers, crayons, or other visuals in the color specifically associated with that quadrant.

4 Purple/Gold	9 Red	2 Pink
3 Green	5 Orange	7 White
8 Blue	1 Black	6 Silver

CHAPTER 5

The Nine Life Areas In Detail

Career & Life Path

Love & Partnership

Family & Foundation

Prosperity & Abundance

Health

Helpful People & Travel

Children & Creativity

Skills & Knowledge

Fame & Aspiration

Exercise: Intention & Goal Bagua

Building on the previous chapter's overview of the Bagua, this chapter goes into greater detail about each of the Nine Life Areas. In creating the foundation of your Feng Shui Life Map, we'll have the opportunity to distinguish the different areas as well as create at least one intention and one goal for each area. By the end of this chapter, these intentions and goals come together to create a complete Intention & Goal Bagua, the frame of your Feng Shui Life Map.

Bagua

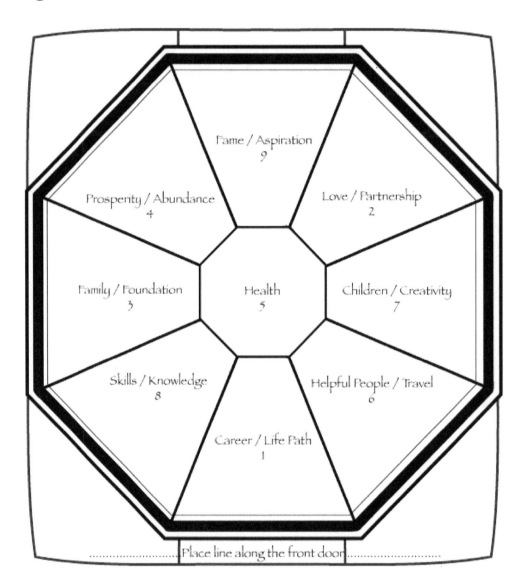

Fame / Aspiration
9

Love / Partnership
2

Prosperity / Abundance
4

Children / Creativity
7

Family / Foundation
3

Health
5

Skills / Knowledge
8

Helpful People / Travel
6

Career / Life Path
1

.... Place line along the front door ....

Career & Life Path

Key Concept	Bliss
Key Action	Follow
Key Intentions	Flow with life easily and effortlessly
	Accept where we are and courageously strive to fulfill our soul's purpose
	Successfully earn a living in a fulfilling way
	Enjoy our current job/career and/or find a new job, our dream job
Associations	Color: Black
	Season: Midwinter
	Time: Midnight
	Body Part: Ears, Kidneys, Bladder
	Shape: Wavy/Irregular
	Element: Water
	Animal: Turtle

Description

The universal Life Force or Chi begins its course through our life starting with our Career & Life Path Area. Here the energy sparks to life our soul, our soul's purpose. The Career & Life Path Area represents both our current job and our dream job, but on a larger scale it represents our **life's path**, the individual **purpose** we have in life. Discovering our Life Path can be a whole life's work!

The key concept here again is **bliss**, because as we patiently and courageously **follow** our bliss, life starts to fall into place. Seemingly insignificant interactions with others become defining moments of who we are and lead us to finding and fulfilling our purpose in life.

We can set intentions here to help us find our ideal job, find new joy in our current job, and discover what it is in life that will fulfill us.

Exercise

Take a moment and consider your intention in Career & Life Path. Ask yourself what's one short-term goal that you can accomplish in the next two weeks to affirm that intention. You can write both your intention and your goal now, or you can just briefly write your goal and go back to apply the full principles of CLEAR & SMART in the following chapters.

- Sample Intention: Have an enjoyable job
- Goal: Write a new resume, go on interviews, or post a resume on Monster.com
- Sample Intention: Become clear on my life path
- Goal: Make a list of five things I want to be when I grow up

_____

_____

_____

_____

_____

_____

Love & Partnership

Key Concept   Openhearted

Key Action   Trust

Key Intentions   Opening our heart to receive and give love fully

                         Finding a partner — intimate, or even business partner

                         Invigorating a current relationship

                         Creating peace between you and another

Associations   Color: Pink

                         Season: Early Autumn

                         Time: Afternoon

                         Body Part: Reproductive organs/organs

                         Shape: Heart!

                         Element: Earth

                         Other: Pairs of things

Description

The Love & Partnership Area represents our most intimate relationships. Harmonious energy flow in this Life Area begins with our unconditionally loving ourselves and then expands out to our spouse, our boyfriend/girlfriend, or partner. As we are **openhearted**, the universe allows us to experience receiving and giving love unconditionally. This requires that we **trust** first ourselves, then the universe, and then others.

It cannot be overstated that this starts when we love and nurture ourselves, when we lovingly fulfill our own needs and desires and affirm that we are worth such in our life. From this place, we can then attract love and partnerships that are balanced and independently healthy rather than fill a void we have not filled within ourselves.

Intentions in this area create an ideal partnership, or they may represent unconditionally loving yourself. Intentions here bring us new partners, as well as help heal, deepen, and reignite our current relationships.

Exercise

Take a moment and consider what your intention might be in Love & Partnership. Ask yourself what's one short-term goal that you can accomplish in the next two weeks to affirm that intention.

- Sample Intention: Start a new intimate relationship
- Goal: Create a profile on match.com
- Sample Intention: Bring romance into my current relationship
- Goal: Plan a romantic date with my partner
- Sample Intention: Love myself unconditionally
- Goal: Do one thing each day to express love to myself

_____

_____

_____

_____

_____

_____

Family & Foundation

Key Concept	Authenticity
Key Action	Accept
Key Intentions	Improving family relationships
	Forgiving and releasing the past
	Feeling secure by meeting basic survival needs of life
	Healing past relationships
Associations	Color: Green
	Season: Spring
	Time: Sunrise
	Body Part: Feet, Liver, Gallbladder
	Shape: Cylindrical, column-like
	Element: Wood
	Animal: Dragon

Description

The Family & Foundation Life Area represents the set of values and beliefs that define who we are as influenced by both blood and surrogate family. It's been said that we become the average of the five people with whom we spend the most time. As these people influence us, our beliefs, our values, our principles for our life are formed.

The key concept here is **authenticity**. As we are authentic, we can easily assess life situations and deem them as beneficial for us or not. The idea is that as we're true to ourselves, we decrease indecision!

Intentions here help us discover and **accept** ourselves. As we accept who we are, we're able to understand that others are who they are because of the influences that have helped shape them. This leads to accepting them, allowing for love and forgiveness, and healing. Intentions here can help us accept ourselves and create healthy familial-type relationships with new and old friends.

Exercise

Take a moment and consider what your intention might be in Family & Foundation. Ask yourself what's one short-term goal that you can accomplish in the next two weeks to affirm that intention.

- Sample Intention: Develop new friendships
- Goal: Join a social organization
- Sample Intention: Make peace with a family member
- Goal: Call that person and have a heart-to-heart

_____

_____

_____

_____

_____

Prosperity & Abundance

Key Concept	Gratitude
Key Action	Giving
Key Intentions	Seeing the glass as half-full
	Cultivating an awareness of the gifts and talents we have
	Feeling blessed, acknowledged, loved
Associations	Color: Purple/Gold
	Season: Late Summer
	Time: Early Morning
	Body part: Hip
	Shape: Coin, five-pointed
	Element: Wood
	Other: Coin-shaped Plants

Description

The Prosperity & Abundance Life Area represents "prosperity" as in money, but more broadly, "prosperity" as in everything that can be experienced abundantly: hugs, chocolate, smiles, laughter. The universe responds abundantly to everything for which we show **gratitude**.

One key to gratitude is perspective. Two people can both have $100, and one will feel wealthy while the other feels poor. It's more fun to be with someone who feels wealthy than someone who feels poor. So, too, as we perceive things to be abundant, we're filled with gratitude. And that gratitude is a magnetic force that attracts more into our lives.

The easiest way to show gratitude is by **giving**. First, giving to ourselves all the things that we need in life. And second, giving to others the things they need. It may sound illogical, but as we give, we're expanding our capacity, creating space, allowing the universe to bring more into our life.

Intentions here help us shift our perspective, recognize abundance, and experience greater prosperity in our lives.

Exercise

Take a moment and consider what your intention might be in Prosperity & Abundance. Ask yourself what's one short-term goal that you can accomplish in the next two weeks to affirm that intention.

- Sample Intention: Become aware of abundance in my life
- Goal: List twenty things I'm grateful for and add five things to that list each day
- Sample Intention: Experience financial freedom
- Goal: Treat myself to one small thing I've been wanting
- Goal: Give away $100 to someone or charity

_____

_____

_____

_____

_____

_____

Health

Key Concept   Vitality

Key Action: Support

Key Intentions   Enjoy physical vitality and emotional well-being

                        Recovering from illness

                        Improving stamina and physical abilities

                        Sleeping better

                        Gaining emotional balance

Associations   Color: Yellow, Orange, Brown/Beige

                        Body Part: Stomach, Spleen

                        Shape: Square, flat, rectangular (long-wise)

                        Element: Earth

Description

The Health Life Area represents our physical as well as emotional health, for our emotions affect how we feel! You'll notice its position in the middle, where it touches every other quadrant. This is indicative of how our health's **vitality** affects every aspect of our lives. The idea here is as we **support** ourselves, and feel supported, we can be supportive to others.

Intentions here can help us perform better physically, get in shape, maintain a healthy diet, or live anxiety free and free from depression.

Exercise

Take a moment and consider what your intention might be in Health. Ask yourself what's one short-term goal that you can accomplish in the next two weeks to affirm that intention.

- Sample intention: Increase my stamina
- Goal: Exercise three times a week
- Sample Intention: Eat healthy
- Goal: Eat one fruit and three vegetables daily
- Sample Intention: Support my partner
- Goal: Give space to express emotions freely, or get up early to go run with him or her

_____

_____

_____

_____

_____

_____

Helpful People & Travel

Key Concept	Synchronicity
Key Action:	Surrender
Key Intentions	Being in synch with life
	Having smooth travel or transitions
	Being treated fairly and in a timely manner
	Creating a strong network of support
Associations	Color: Silver/Gray
	Season: Early Winter
	Time: Evening
	Body Part: Head
	Shape: Round, arc, curved
	Element: Metal

Description

The Helpful People & Travel Life Area represents our moving out into the world to connect with others, traveling, not only the trips abroad such as to Paris, but also at the mundane level of traveling down a particular aisle in a grocery store.

The key concept is **synchronicity**, for when we're in synch with life, we can travel with ease through any situation, **surrendering** to whatever life brings us, knowing that we're fully supported, and whomever happens across our path is there to further us along in life in some way. We're able to trust and follow our intuition as if being guided by angels. In fact, many people place angels in this area of their map and home to represent the idea of angels guiding them through life.

Intentions here help us find the helpful people we need in our life, such as accountants, lawyers, doctors, to build a complete support network, as well as help us travel smoothly and in synch in the world both overseas and throughout our home villages.

Exercise

Take a moment and consider what your intention might be in Helpful People & Travel. Ask yourself what's one short-term goal that you can accomplish in the next two weeks to affirm that intention.

- Sample Intention: Have a smooth and easy trip
- Goal: Meditate in gratitude for five minutes before each stage of the trip
- Sample Intention: Have good health care
- Goal: Find a good doctor

_____

_____

_____

_____

_____

_____

Children & Creativity

Key Concept	Limitless
Key Action	Express
Key Intentions	Being joyful and playful
	Increasing creativity
	Resolving issues involving children
	Successfully launching a new project
	Feeling younger
Associations	Color: White
	Season: Autumn
	Time: Night
	Body Part: Mouth
	Element: Metal
	Animal: Tiger

Description

The Children & Creativity Life Area represents children, both figuratively and literally. If your goal is to have a child, this would be the place to support that reality. It also represents our inner child. And intentions here can help us **express** our inner child's sense of wonder, that feeling of playfulness and invincibility that comes when we approach something with fresh energy. It's our being our own "partner in crime," taking time to do goofy things, as well as giving ourselves, and others, space to **express** our creativity freely.

This is the area that connects us with the infinite possibilities the universe has to offer, unblocking ourselves and moving us beyond places we feel stuck. Intentions here can bring that new project or idea into creation. Intentions here help us develop our creativity, reconnect with our sense of wonder, and conceive something new, both figuratively and literally.

Exercise

Take a moment and consider what your intention might be in Children & Creativity. Ask yourself what's one short-term goal that you can accomplish in the next two weeks to affirm that intention.

- Sample intention: Become more playful and restore my sense of wonder

- Goal   Go on a play date — play on a swing set, skip down a street, or visit a museum

- Sample Intention: Express my creativity in a blog

- Goal: Write one paragraph each day and post it online

_____

_____

_____

_____

_____

Skills & Knowledge

Key Concept   Cultivation

Key Action   Freedom

Key Intentions   Taking time to recharge

Reflecting and developing spiritually

Getting good grades in school

Learning quickly and applying this wisdom to succeed

Associations   Color: Blue

Season: Late Winter

Time: Predawn

Body Part: Hand

Element: Earth

Description

The energy has been built up and expressed, and it's time now to step back, allowing the energy to go to the Skills & Knowledge Area. This area represents the Skills & Knowledge we have acquired in life as well as those that we wish to acquire and develop further.

The Skills & Knowledge Life Area is about reflecting on what we've been through in life, taking it all in and evaluating it, meditating on it, going into Buddha-mind and from that grounded and centered place, devising a **cultivation** plan for **where** we wish to go, **what** we wish to accomplish, **who** we wish to become.

The idea is to allow ourselves the **freedom** to explore those things that interest us, the freedom to change who we are, as well as allowing others the same freedom to explore and change.

Intentions here help us learn new things and skills, and as we practice reflection and meditation, develop the ability to remain calm and centered in all life situations.

Exercise

Take a moment and consider what your intention might be in Skills &
Knowledge. Ask yourself what's one short-term goal that you can
accomplish in the next two weeks to affirm that intention.

- Sample Intention: Learn to speak Italian
- Goal: Cominci una classe italiana!
- Sample Intention: Respond rather than react to the chaos of life
- Goal: Develop a daily meditation practice

_____

_____

_____

_____

_____

_____

Fame & Aspiration

Key Concept	Projection
Key Action	Promise
Key Intentions	Raising self-esteem and self-respect
	Improving reputation
	Clarifying our vision for our future
Associations	Color: Red
	Season: Midsummer
	Time: Midday
	Body Part: Eyes, Heart, Small Intestines
	Shape: Triangle
	Element: Fire

Description

The Fame & Aspiration Life Area represents our fame, as in what we're famous for, in essence, our reputation. This area represents how our image is **projected** both in how we're currently known and in how we'd like to become known, our aspirations.

The key to a good reputation is to be accountable in word, thought, and deed, coming from a place of personal integrity. For this reason, I think of this area as starting with a **promise** — first to ourselves and then to others. What is our promise, that which we're going to hold ourselves accountable to in order to create our desired reputation? From that promise, we can set intentions to define how we wish to be known.

Fame & Aspiration is different from Career & Life Path, although people may think they want their career to be a singer and they want to be known as a singer. Career & Life Path is more about the things that you are **doing** (the gigs, the practice, the auditions, and **the path** to becoming a singer), whereas Fame & Aspiration is more about how we wish to be known/recognized (the awards, the albums, the brilliant reviews, the completed tasks).

Exercise

Take a moment and consider what your intention might be in Fame & Aspiration. Ask yourself what's one short-term goal that you can accomplish in the next two weeks to affirm that intention.

- Sample Intention: Be known as a great cook
- Goal: Create a memorable dinner party
- Sample Intention: Become a recognized actor
- Goal: Audition for a play or film

_____

_____

_____

_____

_____

_____

Exercise: Intention and Goals Bagua

Rewrite your mini-intentions and short-term goals for each Life Area in the Bagua.

Intentions and Goals Bagua

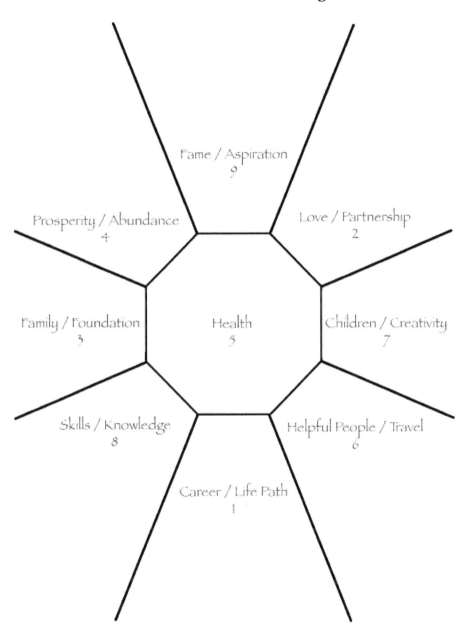

Fame / Aspiration
9

Prosperity / Abundance
4

Love / Partnership
2

Family / Foundation
3

Health
5

Children / Creativity
7

Skills / Knowledge
8

Helpful People / Travel
6

Career / Life Path
1

Intentions and Goals Bagua

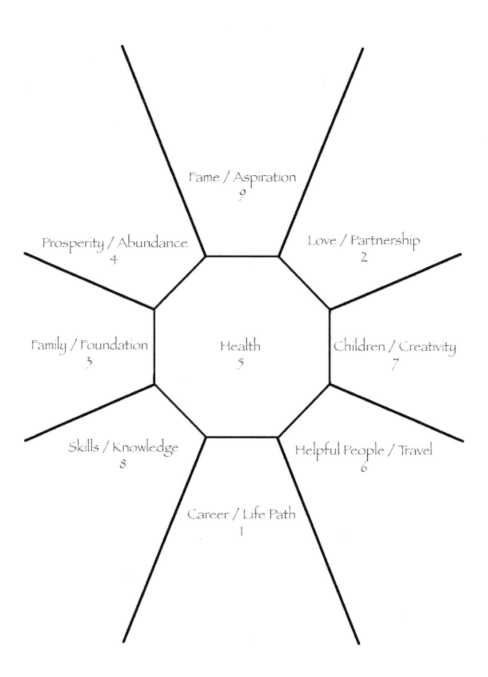

CHAPTER 6

Creative Visualization

This chapter explores the powerful technique known as Creative Visualization. We'll discuss how to develop one's skill with this amazing tool and share the one key step in using it successfully — applying the emotional component. By the end of this chapter, you'll be ready to empower your dreams to becoming manifest!

Creative Visualization

The technique of Creative Visualization involves imagining a desired reality as though it were already real. As our imagination creates a powerful image of a specific reality, our subconscious tunes into this image. And as the subconscious knows no limitation, it begins to believe this reality as true. As a result, the subconscious directs our attention to evidence of that imagined reality in our conscious life. Soon, we find we find ourselves on a path toward manifesting the imagined reality simply by following signs of evidence, which brings us into contact with new people, situations, objects that affirm and propel us to a new reality.

A new reality is just
one thought away!

What we believe we see is generally what we see. And remember, there are always two sides to any coin! If we train ourselves to see the other side of the coin, we can change our thoughts, and in doing so, we change our whole reality.

Creative Visualization was scientifically proven on Olympic athletes who were divided into groups in which they varied the time they spent training physically and the time they spent visualizing their performance. In the end, the athletes who spent more of their time training visually outperformed those who spent more time training more physically.

Just as tennis players may mentally imagine the perfect serve over and over, training and developing their muscle memory to execute that serve, we can train and develop our minds to believe and pursue a particular reality.

The power of thought is much greater than we can imagine! Simply holding a thought in mind sends out an energy that those around us pick up. And as they are affected by our thought-energies, they are compelled to join us in our cause, magnifying the energy until we've created a shift in consciousness of all humanity.

All this begins with a simple thought, one imagined, powerful thought!

Developing imagination

Our imagination is a powerful tool that we begin developing as children. Some cultures and environments encourage the development of imagination, and some stunt the natural desire to fantasize and dream.

Imagination develops like a muscle and needs to be exercised to grow stronger.

The good news is that imagination can be developed wherever you are currently! The first thing to do is give yourself permission to dream, give yourself permission to daydream and fantasize. The more you do so, the more the imagination develops.

Begin exercising this powerful tool! When you first wake up in the morning, spend a few minutes imagining what your day is going to be like and allow yourself to dream big, silly, extravagant things.

> Imagine you just won the lottery, what will you do with all that money?

> Imagine you just discovered you have the ability to fly, where will you go?

> Imagine you just found the cure to a major disease, how will it change the world?

> Imagine you just woke up the king or queen of a country.

> Imagine you just woke up two hundred years in the future.

Spend a few minutes now imagining these and more possibilities. And each day give yourself permission to spend the opening moments of the day exercising your imagination.

How to practice Creative Visualization

Creative Visualization is a technique that involves fully imagining a particular reality by using all of our senses: How does it smell? How does it feel? How does it look? What does it sound like? What does it taste like? Engage all five of our senses to develop a fully formed picture of the reality.

Imagine how each of the five senses will respond.

If I wish to be a singer, I would imagine myself singing, and imagine the stage, the lights, the sound system, the audience, the heat, the smell . . . in as much detail as possible.

> The more **deeply** I immerse myself this imagination, the greater the possibility of it becoming manifest in my life.

> The more **frequently** I immerse myself in this imagination, the quicker it becomes manifest in my life.

Part of the power of a Feng Shui Life Map is that it provides a clear visual image, which easily immerses us deeply into our imagined reality, and as we can place it somewhere to see it often, it increases the frequency we are immersed as well.

Key to successful Creative Visualization

Now that we know how to practice Creative Visualization, I'd like to share the one essential element of Creative Visualization that's the key to its success: emotion.

Emotion powers
Creative Visualization!

When we practice Creative Visualization, it's the emotion that we feel during the visualization that gives it the power to activate the Law of Attraction and begin being made manifest in our life.

How does the visualization make you feel emotionally? Happy? Satisfied? Grateful? Proud? It's the passion that we feel when we visualize our goal happening that gives it the power to manifest. The mind creates the engine, and the emotion gives us the fuel to make it run.

Exercise – Adjective Bagua

Keeping in mind that it's the feeling that fuels the power of the Law of Attraction, I'd like for you to go back now and look at your Intention and Goals Bagua, and for each of the Nine Life Areas come up with at least one adjective that describes how you feel when you imagine that reality being made manifest. It could be "pleased," "confident," "free," or a multitude of other adjectives. You may have more than one adjective for each area, and that's OK, write them both down. You may use the same adjective more than once, that's OK, too!

Adjective Bagua

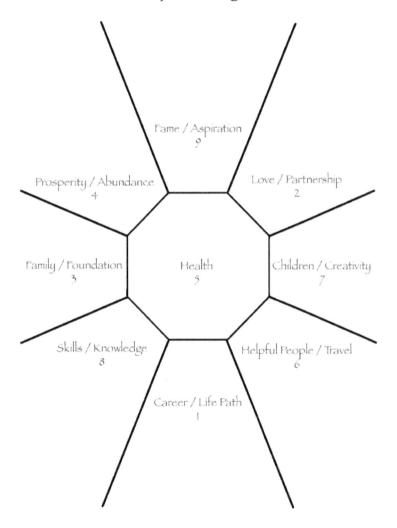

Adjective Bagua

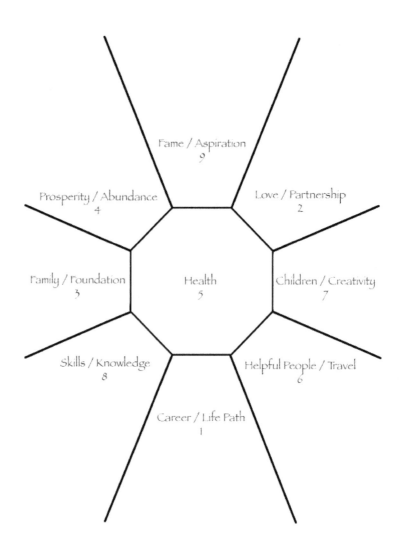

Fame / Aspiration
9

Prosperity / Abundance
4

Love / Partnership
2

Family / Foundation
3

Health
5

Children / Creativity
7

Skills / Knowledge
8

Helpful People / Travel
6

Career / Life Path
1

CHAPTER 7

Vision Boarding

In this chapter, we'll explore the art and process of creating a Vision Board. Because it's built on a Feng Shui Bagua, we get to call ours a Feng Shui Life Map! We'll discuss how a Vision Board works and why it's so powerful. Once you're ready to create your Vision Board, you'll be ready to transform the work you've done in the previous chapters to create your very own visual representation and perpetual affirmation of your dream life. Included in this chapter are the steps necessary to activate your Vision Board to bring to life your dreams.

Going Visual!

For many people, just having created CLEAR Intentions and setting SMART Goals is farther than they've ever been, and they'll notice changes in their lives and feel complete. But I wish to encourage everyone to have some fun and play a little as we take our written goals and adjectives Baguas to the next step and create a Vision Board, a visual representation of our dream lives.

Why visual?

I'm a visual learner. When I see a name written down, I know that I'm much more likely to remember that person's name than if he or she were to say it to me. So I naturally thought that visuals are more effective and thought that's why creating a visual image of an affirmation is more effective than simply having a verbal affirmation. And then I did some research!

Did you know that visual processing engages the largest part of our brain? Processing visual information exercises the visual cortex. Hence the reason Visual Affirmations are so effective is that this huge area is already familiar with doing heavy exercise. By tapping into this developed area of visual processing to begin imagining new realities, we're jumping on a moving train!

Visual symbolism

The key to creating a Vision Board is to think visual and think visual representation. You can create your collage with **specific images** that you have in mind or using visuals that represent **broad concepts**. And remember, if you don't find the image you're looking for, you can draw that image or word in with a marker or crayon or pen or pencil.

Maybe I'd like a new job, which could be represented by a desk, a butterfly, or the word "new." Or if the feeling I get, the adjective I wrote down as my emotional response to getting that new job, is joy, it could be represented by a kid in a bath, or a big smile, or someone laughing.

Maybe I simply wish to get "unstuck," which could be represented by an open door.

Or maybe I wish to know my path, which could be represented by the path in a forest or the image of a long highway.

Here are a few visual representations I have seen on Feng Shui Life Maps:

- Career & Life Path — a desk, a microphone, a typewriter, a path in the woods, a highway

- Love & Partnership — a candlelit dinner table, kissing lips, hands clasped together, hands shaking, wedding rings

- Family & Foundation — family tree, a house, a social scene, or dinner table

- Prosperity & Abundance — an ice cream sundae, diamonds, raised hands in thanks, gold, stacks of money, coins, a safe

- Health — a fit body, a balanced meal, a piece of broccoli, a person doing exercise, a blissed–out yogi

- Helpful People & Travel — a lawyer or doctor, the Eiffel Tower, London Bridge, the globe, a suitcase

- Children & Creativity — the first sprout of a plant, a puppy, a blackboard, a typewriter/computer, seeds

- Skills & Knowledge — a Spanish book, someone in lotus position meditating, graduating ceremonies, degrees

- Fame & Aspiration — an Oscar, a piano, two people hugging, Madonna, a podium

Collage process

The first step to creating a collage is to give yourself permission to be messy and creative, and to have fun! A number of artists have developed collage into a high-art form, displaying their works in major art galleries and selling their art for huge sums of money. Good for them! I'm here to assure you that it doesn't matter how generic, basic, or simple your collage is. The power of a Feng Shui Life Map comes from your combining your intentions with visuals.

One hazard to watch for while doing a collage is getting caught up reading articles or lost in the photos. I find this especially tempting when using magazines like *People* or *Us Weekly* with lots of celebrity news. It's OK if you get distracted, but come back to the process as quickly as possible to prevent delaying the finished project!

Three steps to creating a Vision Board

1. Give yourself twenty-five minutes to collect images!

The process of creating Vision Boarding works well if you start by giving yourself a time limit to collect images and sort through magazines. I suggest setting an alarm to go off! Stop looking for images after the timer goes off, and put the magazines aside and turn to your scrap stack. You can go back after you've done your collage and look for more images if you need to do so.

The idea is to keep yourself moving. Without a deadline, you may find you want to keep searching until you find the exact image you have in your head. I've noticed that those who work in visual arts, such as painters and graphic designers, are especially prone to this. So set the timer! And remember that you can always draw in the images you're looking for using markers, crayons, or pens and pencils.

2. Tear out the WHOLE PAGE if an image appeals to you.

As you flip through a magazine, whenever an image appeals to you, rip out the whole page and set it aside to create a stack of pages, called scrap. You may not use all of the images. Some images you find may inspire you to find other images, or you may end up combining images you hadn't thought of using together.

It's important to remind yourself that you don't have to use every image that you select. I recommend being ready to throw out images or, better yet, keep the scrap stack in a folder for use on your next Vision Board!

3. Collage for twenty-five minutes.

Collage making is easiest when the collecting of images and collage-making parts are separated rather than looking for an image, placing it, and then looking for the next. So, after you've spent twenty-five minutes collecting images, put the magazines aside and start cutting, ripping, shearing the images from the pages and begin laying them out on a Bagua as you feel inspired. If you find you didn't get all the images you needed, give yourself another ten minutes to collect more images.

Some people may benefit from using the Internet to get a specific image, like a particular award that you're hoping to win or the logo of company you wish to work for, and print the image out. This can be a bit like cheating, and quite frankly, it takes longer, but you'll get the specific images you need.

Skilled graphic designers may even find it fun to use a design program such as Illustrator to collect their images and create their collage all digitally. This allows for resizing and layering. However, it's easy to get lost in the technical side and miss some of the pure creativity of using the magazines at hand! So, for your first collage, stick to hands-on with magazines and markers!

You don't have to stay inside the lines!

The Bagua is a guide, and only a guide! Not only can you go outside the lines, you can go off the page!!! You may use a picture to cover two areas or straddle two areas, or have a quote spread across the whole Bagua. You can even start with one single image behind the whole map as a foundation, like a photo of an Oscar, a celebrity you admire, or Mount Everest. And maps can come alive as you combine images with words and drawings.

I recommend using a new, blank sheet of paper or blank Bagua rather than the one you used to write out your goals and adjectives on, such as the Intention and Goals Bagua and Adjective Bagua at the end of chapters 5 and 6. This way, you can go back and review those Baguas later.

Supplies you may need

- Magazines
- Newspapers
- Newsletters
- Printouts from the Internet
- Scissors
- Tape or glue
- Markers
- Crayons
- Pens and pencils
- Blank Bagua to use as foundation
- Colored paper
- An alarm clock or timer
- Permission to have fun!

Activating your Feng Shui Life Map

Once you've finished your Feng Shui Life Map, there are three steps to activate it and take the power of your Life Map to a new level.

First: Share it with people you know. Sharing is a vital step in this process. The power of shared intention will attract things tenfold faster into your life.

- Get together with your best friend, roommate, mentor, or teacher, and go through each of the Nine Life Areas, telling him or her what your goal is and what the image represents.

- Find someone who will allow you to talk and not offer criticism.

Second: Display your Feng Shui Life Map somewhere that you'll see it often. The idea here is to increase the **frequency** you meditate on the images, creating new thought-habits, new neural patterns that ultimately lead to attracting whatever is necessary to manifest your dream life.

- Make photocopies of it and hang it in several places.

- Frame it and make it a conversational piece of art in your home.

- Take a photo of it and use it as your phone or computer screen saver.

Third: Create a reflection of your intention in your environment.

- First, create space for the new thing you desire.

- Second, place an object in the area of your space that correlates to that area of the Bagua. Use anything that evokes the passion you feel or reminds you of the goal you have as a reflection of your intention.

Next: Try creating a Feng Shui Life Map for the next year of your life!

Exercise – Feng Shui Life Map

It's time to make your Feng Shui Life Map!

In the previous chapters, we discussed all the elements and processes for creating a clear and balanced foundation for your life and mapping this out on a Feng Shui Bagua. Here we now have a chance to pull all the elements together to create a Feng Shui Life Map, which is a visual representation and perpetual affirmation of your dream life.

Follow these steps to create a Feng Shui Life Map:

1. Create a CLEAR Intention and SMART Goal in each of the Nine Life Areas — write these intentions and goals on a Bagua in the individual Life Areas. You can use the Intentions and Goals Bagua you created in chapter 5.

2. Using Creative Visualization, chose 1–3 adjectives that describe the way you would feel (emotionally) when your goal becomes manifest, and write these adjectives in the Life Areas of your Bagua. You can use the Adjective Bagua you created in chapter 6.

3. Create a Vision Board choosing images that represent the intention, the goal, and the adjectives you have in each of the Nine Life Areas.

4. Activate your completed Feng Shui Life Map:

    • Share it with someone you trust

    • Display it somewhere you see it often

    • Create one reflection for each of the Life Areas in your environment

Remember!!! It's essential that you activate your Feng Shui Life Map. Activating it will help manifest your desired reality many times faster!

Intention and Goals Bagua

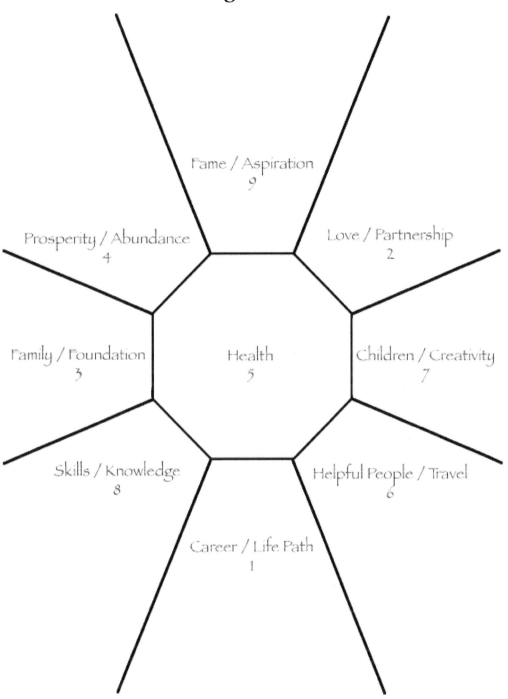

Fame / Aspiration
9

Prosperity / Abundance
4

Love / Partnership
2

Family / Foundation
3

Health
5

Children / Creativity
7

Skills / Knowledge
8

Helpful People / Travel
6

Career / Life Path
1

Adjective Bagua

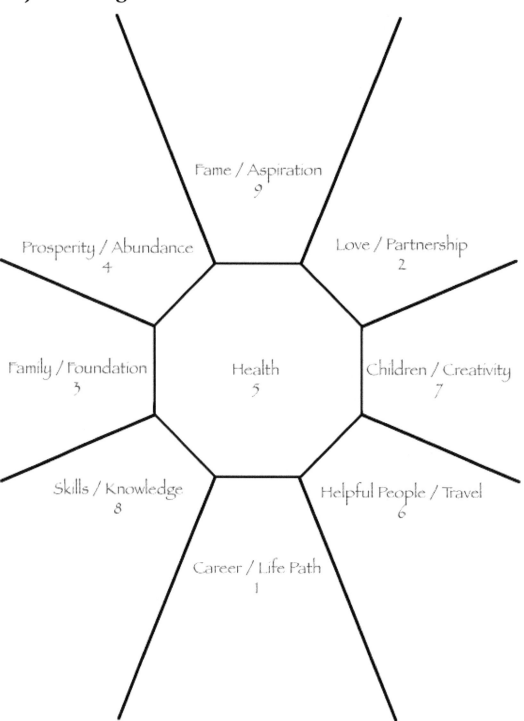

Fame / Aspiration
9

Prosperity / Abundance
4

Love / Partnership
2

Family / Foundation
3

Health
5

Children / Creativity
7

Skills / Knowledge
8

Helpful People / Travel
6

Career / Life Path
1

Bagua

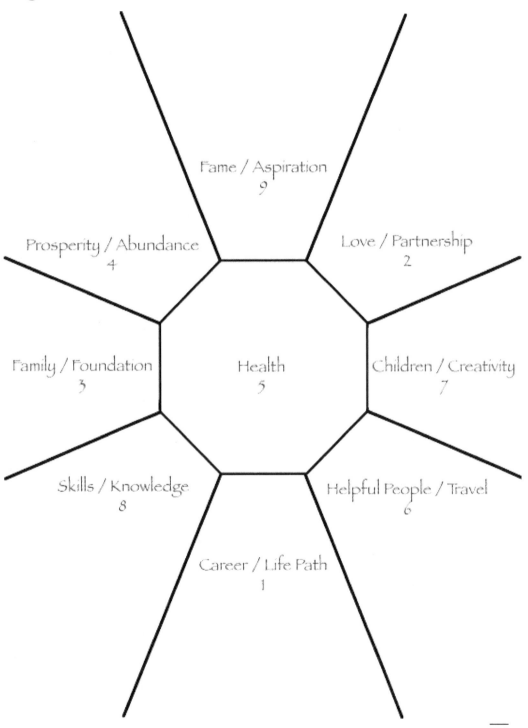

Fame / Aspiration
9

Prosperity / Abundance
4

Love / Partnership
2

Family / Foundation
3

Health
5

Children / Creativity
7

Skills / Knowledge
8

Helpful People / Travel
6

Career / Life Path
1

Bagua

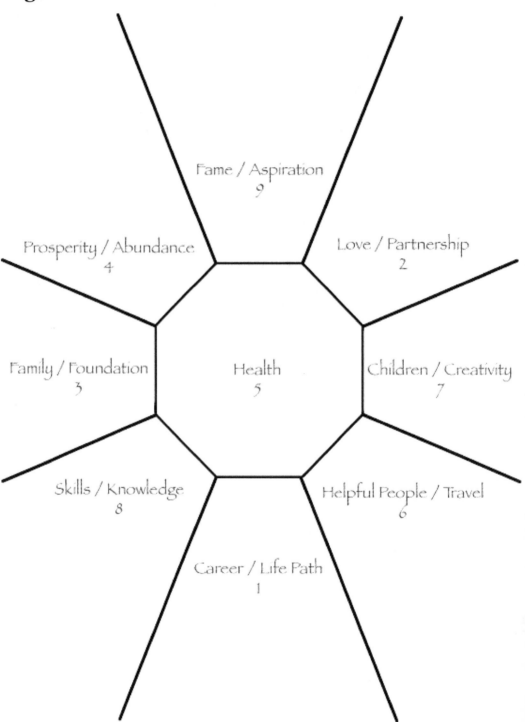

Fame / Aspiration
9

Prosperity / Abundance
4

Love / Partnership
2

Family / Foundation
3

Health
5

Children / Creativity
7

Skills / Knowledge
8

Helpful People / Travel
6

Career / Life Path
1

PART IV

Creating
a Supportive Environment

Embrace Simplicity!

CHAPTER 8

Feng Shui Life Mapping for Your Home and Office

This chapter introduces many of the basic principles of Feng Shui as well as their practical application within your home and work environments. The most important and powerful factor in creating a supportive environment is in creating proper reflections of your intentions. Using intention, feel free to employ these Feng Shui tips and suggestions to enhance your home and office and enhance the use of your Feng Shui Life Map.

Introduction

I've included this section as a collection of key elements to consider when working with Feng Shui in your home and office.

Keep in mind that there are numerous schools of Feng Shui that began forming centuries ago, coming to the United States in a Westernized form in the late twentieth century. My approach to Feng Shui is based in this Westernized form, as it's the most easily applicable to the American household and mind-set.

To use Feng Shui, place the Bagua over the floor plan of the house, with the bottom of the Bagua lined up with the main entrance. This allows you to easily determine what area of the home, and what area of each individual room, corresponds to which specific Life Area. With the Bagua, you can then look at this area to see what's reflecting your intention, as well as what may be impeding your intention by reflecting poor intentions.

The following sections give tips for creating positive Chi Flow. Enjoy!

Rooms with a purpose!

"Closets are for clothes" was one of my college roommate's favorite T-shirts. One day he was wearing his shirt in a restaurant, and the waiter read it and responded, "Well, of course closets are for clothes, kitchens are for cooking!" The hidden message was lost, but the point was poignant in terms of Feng Shui.

Bedrooms are for sleeping. Living rooms are for living. Dining rooms are for dining. And so on! In smaller spaces, rooms sometimes do double duty, serving as the living room, family room, TV/entertainment room, office and meditation/yoga area. But the more we dedicate a space to a particular energy **when we are engaged in that activity**, the more successful that energy can support us in our efforts.

With that in mind, whenever possible, avoid dual-purpose uses of space. And whenever you need to double up on a room's energetic use, create a clear break, a clean separation between the activities, by clearing up after the first activity before beginning the next.

For example, if you use your dining room table as your desk, clear everything work-related off the table before eating. (Otherwise, you're eating your work!) If your living room doubles as your laundry room, clear the laundry before crashing on the couch to watch TV or hanging out with others.

Room and house shapes

The ideal shape of a space (room, home, or office) is a perfect square. Shapes that diverge from this have various pluses and minuses. Unusually shaped spaces give a creative twist to the Flow of Energy, but they aren't cause for alarm! The energy is still moving! The trick is to work with the space to reap the benefits of its shape while mitigating any of its potential challenges.

Common deviations from a square, such as an L shape or U shape, may provide a "bonus" area. If the wall from which the space juts out is more than two-thirds complete, it's a bonus! If the wall is less than two-thirds complete, then it's considered a "missing quadrant," and cures can be applied to bring the missing piece back into the space.

Such cures include placing a mirror on the wall where the "missing quadrant" would be to visually give the illusion of the space being there. If you can access the area outside the "missing quadrant," you can place something that creates an energetic boundary where the wall would have been. Such items to use include a plant, a light (pointed toward the house), a crystal either hanging or buried, or anything that feels like an appropriate boundary to you. See "Cures" later in this chapter for tips on using cures.

The same rule of thirds applies to any area being treated to Feng Shui: your desk, the closet, the backyard, the whole lot, and so forth.

Clutter and maintenance

Often, when people think of Feng Shui, they first think about their need to clear their clutter. True!

The external reflects the internal.

External order and harmony reflect internal order and harmony. External clutter and chaos reflect internal clutter and chaos.

But more profoundly, the external **influences** the internal. When your environment is healthy, it affects you positively. When it's unhealthy, it's going to affect you negatively.

Anything unused, unloved, or unfinished is clutter!

The average American rarely uses more than half of his or her belongings. And basically, anything that's unused, unloved, or left unfinished creates sticky, heavy energy. This energy causes stress in our life by distracting our attention and gobbling up the energy we could be using to deal with other things.

All parts of the home or office are important, but Feng Shui places special emphasis on the big three: bedroom, kitchen, and entrance. We'll spend some time on each of these next. But first, let's get in a clutter-clearing mind-set!

Clutter carries emotional baggage!

One challenge we face with clearing clutter is all the emotional energy attached to it. Clearing clutter is something akin to therapy where we're required to make a decision, finish something we've been avoiding (possibly for a reason), or discard of something along with all the emotional energy attached to it.

To mitigate this challenge I have three suggestions:

- First, have in mind a clear idea of what it is that you wish to manifest in your life, the thing you're clearing space for in your life. Clearly visualize this thing in as much detail as possible.

- Second, divorce yourself from your objects! Observe yourself in the act of clearing the clutter, and note when you feel emotions come up. Acknowledge, "ah, there's a strong emotion attached to this object," and let go of it by reminding yourself what it is that you're creating space for in your life. Another way to do this is to get help — a friend or professional who can objectively review items you've collected from a detached perspective. For example: hold a fashion show for your friends and get a thumbs-up or thumbs-down on any clothes that you're waffling about.

- Third, approach clutter clearing in small stages! Don't tackle the messiest part of your home first, start with a simple spot so you can experience success. In fact, I highly suggest clearing only one place at a time and then taking a break. Even if you feel you have the energy to do more, stop and create a clear break in the process. Go for a walk or start fresh the next day.

Clear clutter in small stages because as we begin to remove clutter in one space, energy begins flowing and we're given a boost! By starting small, we free up more and more bits of energy so that we have ample energy to tackle that "big project" we've been saving for last.

Light, color, air

Clean air, natural light, and comforting colors are necessary elements of a healthy environment. And the best possible situation is for all of them to be harmonious. Too much or too little will create imbalance.

Clean air can be brought in by using an air purifier, an open window to an unpolluted air source, or even through essential oil diffusers and humidifiers. If using fans or purifiers, be certain the filters are cleaned regularly.

We're living in a fortunate time when "natural light" can be simulated through the use of full-spectrum light bulbs available at most hardware stores. In the event that natural light is not flowing in, such as in basement apartments, use one of these fantastic bulbs and set it on a timer to simulate a few hours of natural light.

Colors are powerful!!! And when choosing "comforting colors," it's good to acknowledge individual tastes and preferences; however, their influence is instantaneous and often universally applicable. Colors used in moderation will maintain balance while providing desired feelings.

Reds and purples increase energy and blues often mellow energy out. Green represents new growth, but too much can evoke feelings of jealousy. Yellows and oranges are associated with health and creativity. Browns and beiges are neutralizing and allow colorful accents to stand out more prominently.

Whatever colors you choose, remember that moderation is key. And keeping a balance of natural light, clean air, and comforting colors will ensure a harmonious foundation from which to build a supportive environment.

Entryway

The entryway is called the "mouth of Chi" because everything that enters into the space enters through the front door. Each doorway in your home or office is important, as they represent the portals through which everything must pass into the room, but the most important door is the front door.

Many people enter their home through the back, side, or garage door. But it's important to make a point of entering through the front door every once in a while. This gives us a chance to view the home as a visitor would, as well as the chance to bring personal energy in through the main entrance.

Everything about the entryway affects how Chi is received into the space. The ideal situation is a pathway that's visually appealing, easily navigated, and is somewhere between a straight path and a maze of twists and turns. The natural element associated with the entrance is water, and so curved and natural winding paths are most auspicious.

Obviously, anything that doesn't uplift energy at the entryway is not beneficial. Dead plants or objects that block the path or view of the door can deter positive Chi from getting to your space. Empty pots, trash cans, or unused tools all send less than inviting messages. And welcome mats can be helpful (they can even say "welcome"), or they can give the wrong image if they are old, torn, mud-caked.

Common entryway challenges:

- If the front door is up a great number of steps, the energy has to climb up (as do your guests). To encourage this climb, use lights, vines that climb up the stairs, or objects that inspire and uplift. One client I worked with had a long stairway to her entrance. To fit with her personality, we put humorous signs along the way to provide visitors the opportunity to rest, laugh, and make it to the top in a lighthearted mood.

- If the front door is down a flight of steps or beneath the street, protection is needed to prevent energy from rushing down into your space. Natural protection is the best, such as plants, but lights that shine up the stairs, a mirror that reflects up, or a mat that creates an energetic barrier also works well.

- If your door is opposite another door, such as in an apartment building, or if there's little to protect your door from the rushing energy of the street, or if there's a large object towering in front of your door, a mirror or reflective surface just above the door can help reflect negative energies away from the space. Traditional Feng Shui tools use convex mirrors in such instances. Convex mirrors are used for protective purposes, as they bubble out and act as a buffer to the world. (Concave mirrors create a condensed and upside-down image, bringing the energy into a single-pointed focus, which may be useful at other times.)

Once inside the door, what's the first thing you see? First impressions are important! Ideally, the first thing a person sees is something inviting, that is, inviting the positive energy in! A pile of disorganized shoes is not as appealing as a small bench where people can sit to take off their shoes and store them underneath.

Additionally, the entryway table needs to be organized, clean, and ideally not so large as to block the path of energy, or so small that it prevents being functional. Finally, the entryway closet is an ideal place to store only the items you're using for that season, with enough room for guests' belongings to make them feel they have a space prepared and waited for them.

The goal is to bring as much positive energy into your space as possible, and the possibilities for creating this are endless. When you view your entryway ask yourself, "How does this reflect my intention for inviting positive energies into my life?" Let your entryway be your unique signpost to the world that you're here, ready to receive all the benefits it has to offer!

Beds and bedrooms

The bedroom is one of the most important rooms in your house because it's where you sleep and, hence, lie unconsciously open to all the energies around you.

The simplest way to summarize where to put the bed and arrange the room is to imagine your bed needing to be protected in every way. The headboard needs a firm, stable wall to rest against. The view from the bed should allow you to easily see all parts of the room. Pathways of energy, entering from doors and windows or hallways, need to be soothed or calmed rather than rushing at the bed. And the mattress and bed frame need to be comfortable and stable.

Wood is the ideal element for the bed frame, for it's grounding and gives the energetic properties of a tree putting down roots. Metal frames can be "cured" energetically by placing a token to symbolize grounding on each corner, by using wooden coasters or tying a red string around the leg or other such item. Four-poster and canopy beds are suitable as long as they're stable and the canopy is in good condition.

The bed also symbolizes your intimate relationships, and thus equality is ideal. The bedside tables or lamps or pillows don't have to match, but having two of each creates an energetic balance between partners and invites someone to share your bed and feel like he or she has a space and place there (and in your life). Ideally, the bed can be accessed from both sides, to allow for two independent people coming together. Single lamps, tables, or pillows energetically affirm being single, which is a perfectly reasonable choice as well.

Nothing goes under the bed! Imagine that whatever you place under the bed becomes the foundation for your dreams as you sleep! Why exhaust yourself during your sleep?! If you have an expensive under-the-bed-storage system because of space, create an energetic boundary beneath the mattress (a solid sheet beneath the mattress or similar item) and keep the storage compartments obsessively tidy and free from clutter.

Let the bedroom be a place of peace!

As the bedroom is the place for rest, anything that amplifies energy must be minimized or mitigated in some way. I had a client who loved her red sheets, but complained she couldn't sleep in them! Red is so powerful and energetic, it's little wonder why!

Mirrors are great to improve the ease of seeing around the room from the bed without having to struggle, but they're very high in energy, and if they're positioned so that when you look up from bed, you catch a glimpse of yourself moving, it can give the unconscious message of someone else in bed — this leads to the feared "mirrors near the bed cause infidelity" syndrome. If your closet is mirrored and is next to the bed, hang curtains to cover it when you're sleeping.

A few plants are OK in the bedroom. There, I said it! I'm not talking about sleeping in an enclosed arboretum, but a plant or two is OK. Yes, plants expire carbon dioxide during the evening hours. They actually do this all the time, but more so at night. But they only expire about as much as a pet would if it slept in the room. Basically, unless you're sleeping in an airtight space, one or two small plants may be a nice addition to the room without causing alarm.

Fans, heaters, air purifiers, and white-noise machines are all energy sources. In urban areas they're often necessary tools for creating quiet. When used, I suggest positioning them so they're not right next to the bed.

TVs in the bedroom are best when they can be hidden in a cupboard, armoire, or something of that nature when not in use. They are huge power sources, and they give the effect of a large black eye staring at you at night when they are left exposed.

Lastly, your bed is a shrine. It's not a place to let laundry pile up, drop book bags or other items, and certainly not the place to do your work. Nurture it as a place of rest and comfort.

Kitchen

The kitchen is like an umbilical cord to the universal energies. Often the kitchen is associated with our health, which is a great analogy for the place where we prepare the food to nourish our bodies.

The fridge, cupboards, and drawers all need to be clean and organized. Food that's expired, unused, or going bad in the fridge is likened to energy in the body that has become stagnant and causing disease. Clean out the fridge every month, taking time to wash down the shelves with the intention of it representing the washing out, cleaning, and purifying of your organ systems.

Broken and unused dishes, utensils, and glassware also present a negative association, as they represent a broken and stagnant energy in the body. Clean out any items no longer in use or broken. And if necessary, buy some new items to affirm your intentions of good health!

The stove is the powerhouse of the home!

And then there's the stove! I like to describe it as the Chi jet engines of your life. Each burner represents an avenue for Chi to come powerfully into your life. For that reason, keeping the burners clean and in excellent working condition is essential. What's more, use a different burner every time you use the stove to reinforce the idea of being open to all possible avenues of abundance and Chi Flow in your life.

Many times, you'll see a mirror or reflective surface behind the stove. This is a Feng Shui trick to symbolically double the amount of Chi jet engines in your life. Instead of four avenues of income, you now have eight! Instead of four new clients, friends, partners, you now have eight!

Most importantly, when we consider the kitchen as a reflection of our health, hold in mind positive and loving energy while working in the kitchen. When you cook, imagine that the meals are infused with the powerful energetic intentions you have while you're preparing them. When you clean, imagine eliminating the unnecessary bits of energy in our lives and allowing for a clean vessel to invite new energies in.

Living room

The living room meets so many diverse needs, from friendly gatherings to romantic moments, from entertainment to quiet and meditation, that it essentially needs to be a comfortable place where energy can disperse evenly and thoroughly.

When you choose furnishings in the living room, keep in mind they need to be of an appropriate size to the overall space. Anything with sharp edges or that juts out into the traffic area creates a negative energetic affect by inducing the feeling of crowding or endangerment. Sharp edges can be softened with fabrics or the placement of other items such as plants. And objects jutting into the main traffic areas need to be rearranged so that flow is comfortably achieved.

As this is often the main area for entertainment, TVs and other electronic devices are common and useful. They generate a great deal of energy, however, and can throw the balance off in the room. Ideally, a TV will be hidden in a cabinet when not in use. If it's not, it's important the TV not be the main focus of the room, with visitors left to stare at it whether or not it's on. Start by creating a conversation area and then add the entertainment components in a way that allows comfortable viewing.

Windows are for looking!

Windows are called the "eyes of the house," as they let you to see out and can symbolize your view of the world. As such, they need to be allowed to open fully, be clean, and remain unblocked by furniture or other items.

Avoid energy tunnel passageways!

Rushing energy is created when the entrance of the living room is opposite a door, patio, or hallway that gives the effect of the energy going in one way and right out the opposite. We want energy to come gently into the room and disperse. To help this happen, arrange furnishings in a way to cause the energy to move around instead of shoot straight through. If furnishings cannot be arranged to do this, use a throw rug with a pleasing design.

The easiest way to approach arranging and creating good energy flow in your living room is to keep coming back to the idea of balance. Balance light and dark, color and neutral, furniture and empty space, entertainment and quiet. When in doubt, start with the bare essentials of seating and lighting and work from there. A few plants, some pleasing and complimentary draperies, a functional and unobtrusive entertainment center all can be added piece by piece until a completely balanced room is achieved.

Bathrooms

Bathrooms are key to the home as a place for rejuvenation and cleansing, and as the source of the powerful natural element: water! The first step to using this power is, as with most places, creating a place that feels comfortable and enhances benefits while mitigating potential drawbacks.

Drains drain!

Drains allow water, and Chi, to leave your home. They are essential, but left open, or clogged or dirty, the energy flow of the house becomes drained, stagnant, or muddy. In addition to keeping drains clean and functional, the best advice is to keep the toilet lid down, the sink drain closed, and the tub drain covered to prevent loss of energy.

The bathroom door should be kept closed, especially if it opens into a bedroom or can be seen from the entrance. If a window is not available to eliminate humidity, a dehumidifier is better than leaving the door open.

If your toilet is on the opposite side of the same wall as the bed or stove, it's highly recommended to create an energetic barrier such as a mirror. Sometimes the mirror can be placed behind the toilet.

Avoid the infinity mirror vortex!

It's a common energetic conundrum of having mirrors on opposite walls facing each other. This allows you to see your back when getting ready, but the effect creates an infinity of energy bouncing back and forth, and stepping into this vortex can be disorienting at the very least. It's better to place mirrors on walls side by side and avoid this.

Bathmats, towels, shower curtains, and wall decor all help create an environment that's comforting and nourishing to the soul. When you select these items, consider balance. As the bathroom already has a great deal of the natural element of water, colors and items added to the bathroom will bring the other natural elements (fire, metal, wood, and earth) into the room to balance the presence of water. Earth, earthenware, earthy colors all help absorb too much water.

An affirmation mirror!

Use your bathroom mirror as a place to post your affirmations. Every time you're brushing your teeth or getting ready, you're consciously and subconsciously amplifying your positive energies! Some of my clients have made a collage around the mirror and others use post-it notes, while others write on the mirror with erasable markers. Whatever you choose, keep the affirmations fresh by changing them up every now and then.

Lot & garden

The Bagua can be applied not only to individual rooms and the home but also to the entire lot as well, including the garden. The shape of the lot influences Chi Flow, as does the location of your home on the lot.

Ideally, the home is slightly to the front of the lot and is balanced all the way around. Additionally, we want supportive elements behind as well as inviting elements in front. The front of the home needs to welcome as well as slow and calm energies approaching the house. And the back needs to be a sanctuary for private energy, with protective natural features such as a mountain or hill, or energetic boundaries such as shrubs, trees, or a fence.

The front of the home being up or down a flight of stairs can affect energy coming peacefully to you. If visitors must climb to get to you, it'll slow much of the positive (and negative) energies. To assist the energy (and your guests) with the climb, use healthy vines climbing up the stairs or lights that shine brightly and encouragingly upward (such as a string of lights along the banister).

If visitors must climb down, too much positive and negative energy may tumble into your home, in which case energetic barriers are needed, such as a convex mirror above your door or a plant or other object that protects and guards the door.

Water fountains at the front entrance are ideal. The natural element of water is associated with the entrance, and the spray of water in a fountain symbolizes a diffusing and calming fount for energies.

A fire pit, barbeque, or other fire feature is excellent for the back, as the natural element of fire is associated with that area. Keep in mind that shapes can also be used to symbolize fire, such as triangles. Many people place their pool in the backyard, lots of water in the fire area! Creating balance is essential. Tiki torches, red pool toys, and even a fire pit area beyond the pool will help mitigate the imbalance.

Gardens provide an amazing source of positive energy for your home. Any size, any shape, and with any items growing will all amplify positive energy for your home and your life. Ideally, a garden will have winding paths to promote a natural feel and natural flow of energy. And it's a given that a garden requires work to maintain, but the effort of keeping it healthy and free from garden tools and debris cannot be overstated.

Office

The office represents your engagement with the world in many ways. You have a special role on this planet, to share a unique and special talent and gift with the world. How you share your gift is reflected by your workspace. And how the world responds will be enhanced, augmented, and fine-tuned by practicing Feng Shui in your office or home office to create a harmonious relationship that's beneficial financially as well as spiritually and emotionally and mentally.

First, let's talk about your home office. The challenge of having a home office is keeping work and home life separate. For this reason, choose a room for the office as far from the bedroom as possible. Additionally, keep the office specifically for office activities solely. If you need to meet with your family, choose a space apart from the office. If your home office is not necessarily a separate room, it's essential to create containment for the supplies and files so that work can be shut off from the rest of the house when you're not "working."

In-boxes are opportunities for abundance, and as such, they should be kept tidy, free of junk mail or unfinished business, and have an organized and welcoming feel. If you look at your in-box and have any negative feelings such as overwhelmed or anxiety or frustration, take steps to address those feelings. Your in-box should give you an "oh boy!" feeling!

Desks are as important to the office as the bed is to the bedroom. Position the desk so that you have what's called a "command position." In this position, you're able to see the door and anything coming in the door with ease. It's best not to center the desk right in front of the door, as that can invite energy to rush right into your work. If you cannot easily see the front door from where you're sitting, because you're facing a wall or different direction, and you can't move the desk, place a mirror somewhere on the desk, computer, or wall that allows you to see the door easily.

Feng Shui your desktop!

Desktops can use Feng Shui, too! Lay the Bagua over the desktop to determine what area of the desktop represents what Life Area and adjust placement of items accordingly. For example, name plates, business cards, and the like do well facing out and placed in the Fame & Aspirations

Area. As with all areas of life, organization and freedom from clutter is essential for projecting a calm and harmonious energy into your (work) world.

Chairs in your office and especially your desk chair need to be sturdy, comfortable, and ideally have a high enough back to allow you to rest easily. Your desk chair is your throne! Be sure that your throne is reflecting the stability, confidence, and power you wish to feel in your position.

Filing cabinets have sharp corners, which could use some softening through the use of well-placed plants or a fabric over them. Additionally, any and all shelves need to be kept closed when not in use to create a greater sense of calm, and metaphorically, keep your client's energy from dissipating.

Ergonomics are not just good for the physical longevity of your body, they also allow you to work without being distracted by physical discomfort. Just as the wrist is below the elbow naturally, when you are using your keyboard or mouse, the wrist should be positioned so that it's still below the elbow's height. When the wrist is higher than the elbow, the shoulder and neck muscles have to stay engaged to type or move the mouse, and this leads to some uncomfortable issues. Finally, the monitor needs to be placed in such as way that you're neither looking up nor down. Use a book under the monitor if you can't adjust it any other way.

For an office outside the home, follow these same tips and focus on creating a comfortable space that invites in energy and allows it to flow naturally. Use mirrors, plants, or other objects to create energetic barriers that slow the flow of energy coming toward your desk, whether from your cubical mate or from the other offices. Ideally, choose a desk and chair (or office) whose previous owner was promoted rather than one from someone who was fired or left upset, as they all hold energetic memory.

Remember the most practical way to apply Feng Shui to any area of your environment is to ask yourself, "How does this space reflect my intention?" Let your office reflect your intention to be successful, financially stable, helpful, as well as any other intentions you may hold.

Feng Shui cures

Cures are those items we can use to adjust the Flow of Energy in one's space to correct stagnant areas, blocked areas, missing areas, and the like. Cures are as much symbolic as they are powerful in their elemental nature.

A guiding principle of Feng Shui is to create balance and harmony. Elementally, this means balancing the five elements of water, wood, fire, earth, and metal in each Life Area. And so the first step in creating any cure is to attempt to create a balance of these elements by adding items according to their constructive and destructive cycles. These cycles enable the energy to increase or decrease according to this formula:

Constructive cycle: Water feeds Wood, Wood feeds Fire, Fire creates Earth, Earth creates Metal, Metal holds water.

Destructive cycle: Water extinguishes Fire, Fire melts Metal, Metal cuts Wood, Wood pierces Earth, Earth dams water.

If a room is predominantly one element, use the destructive cycle formula to add items that will balance out that element. Additionally, add items that'll feed or fuel creating the missing element. For example: in the bathroom, there's a lot of water, so it's useful to add earth to absorb some of the water (destructive cycle), add fire to help nourish and create earth (constructive cycle), and avoid wood, which pierces earth and may deplete the necessary earth element.

Colors can be a fun and simple way to work with the elements. The elemental associations are

- Black with water,

- Green with wood (tree),

- Red with fire,

- Brown with earth, and

- Silver/Gray with metal.

Symbolism, by its very nature and cultural meaning, gives power to a variety of items: Native Americans use dream-catchers, Celtics use knots, and Christianity has the iconic symbol of the cross. Just as each of these cultures offer an internationally renowned symbolic image or tool, Chinese Feng Shui practices have brought us tools such as bamboo flutes, Fu-Dogs, Bagua mirrors, red tassels and crystal spheres.

Using Chinese Feng Shui tools in an effort to invoke their traditional power can be as effective as stumbling on a magic wand or as haphazard as wearing a rabbit's foot because someone said it was "lucky." My advice is to use symbolic images and tools that resonate with you and your style.

I have had numerous clients who confess to me their fear of having placed their Fu-Dog facing the incorrect direction. If a power tool is connected with fear and anxiety, it's going to promote fear and anxiety! Select a "cure" that you already feel a kinship with, whether it's a plant, a colorful drawing made by your nephew, a magnet in the shape of the Eiffel Tower, or crystals, tassels, and Fu-Dogs.

Keep in mind a few suggestions when selecting items to use as cures in your space. First, your intention infused into the tool is more powerful than the tool. It isn't the rabbit's foot that's lucky, it's believing you're lucky! Second, be certain that whatever you use is in good condition. It's best not to have broken statues or chipped crystals or scratched, faded, old mirrors. Third, "bless" the cure once it's been placed by envisioning its beneficial effects on the situation you're curing.

Some power tools that you may wish to employ as cures:

Living items. Anything living brings life! A pet, a plant, a fishbowl, fresh flowers, and the like will bring more living energy into a space.

Light. Light brings energy! Simply adding a lamp, a row of garden lights, or reflective surfaces to increase light will increase Chi Flow.

Electronics. Anything powered by electricity is a symbolic source of power in your home. Fans, air purifiers, disco balls, entertainment equipment add energy. Use with caution so as not to add too much energy and throw off the balance of peace versus activity.

Crystals. Every crystal has a unique purpose. Consult with a professional before amassing crystals in one area or another. Best rule of thumb, as silly as it sounds: when crystal hunting, let the crystal call out to you.

Mirrors. Mirrors represent water, reflect negative energy, expand and double the space, and provide a host of aesthetic benefits. Sometimes it seems a mirror can cure everything, but too many mirrors can cause a lot of unneeded energy as well! Maintain balance.

Sound. Sound can calm energies or augment energies as needed. Chimes are a classic use of natural sound enhancement. Additional sound therapy can be created from sound machines, radios, TVs, and the like.

Water. Water is a powerful energy source, and fountains, fishbowls, water plants, and objects associated with water such as wavy symbols or the color black all help to bring in this powerful element. One suggestion, limit water in the Love & Partnership Area, as it can create emotional situations.

Weight. If you feel the need to be grounded or increase your foundation in an area of your life, you can use images and objects with some heft to them. Stones, actual weights, and large heavy pots provide this beautifully.

Fragrance. Smell is powerful! Diffusers, fresh flowers, perfumes, and incense all create a normalizing of the energy and promote various desired feelings.

Touch. We are tactile beings! Objects that are pleasing to the touch can enhance our feeling of comfort. Soft fabrics on couches, or even items that appear soft to the touch, offer a calming, healing energy.

While these are some commonly associated power tools, remember that anything that's personally meaningful to you can be used with intention to create healing as a cure and to enhance an environment.

Energy cleansing and blessing

Objects are made up of energy, and as such, they have energetic memory. These traces of past energies with which they have come into contact cling to them much the way a fragrance of someone you hug clings to you even after you've said good-bye. These energies need to be cleansed from the objects to prevent buildup and, more importantly, to prevent the residual energies from affecting your environment.

On numerous occasions during a home or work consultation, I'm attracted to a particular item. Upon investigation, my clients will tell me the person who gave them that item was crazy or did something unforgivable or had caused an unpleasant experience in their lives. The object itself is a reminder of this unpleasantness and for that reason alone should be given the heave-ho. But a greater reason to consider removing or cleansing the object is that the negative energies associated with the item are leeching into the environment.

Different practitioners practice various cleansing and blessing rituals, and I would encourage creating your own unique way to perform such ceremonies. The ceremonies I use are ones I've learned from various spiritual guides over the years.

- Water is amazing at energy clearing. Holding the object beneath a clean running water source is ideal. Alternatively, dipping the object in a large body of water such as the sea or ocean provides extra cleansing, as the salt is a powerful cleanser as well.

- Sage and other incense can cleanse and bless an object by physically clearing the energy fields around the object. Dried white sage is a favorite, but any fragrance, used with intention, will work.

- Bells neutralize energies. A wonderful technique called "toning" in which a bell, instrument, or other musical item, including your voice, can be employed to essentially calm and restore an object's energy to a baseline. Chanting Om is an easy option here.

Keep in mind that any ritual in which your intention is to clear the energy and bless the object will be effective.

Cleansing and blessings are recommended whenever an object is moved, gifted, or repaired. Whenever I complete a consultation, I ask my client to perform such a ceremony to reintroduce his or her own energies throughout the space and welcome any changes that were created.

The most important aspect of any ceremony is attitude. A smile filled with love will conquer a host of difficult energies. ☺

Conclusion

Congratulations!!!

It is an honor to have shared with you this powerful tool called Feng Shui Life Mapping. Again, I wish to encourage you to see your first Feng Shui Life Maps as opportunities to learn the technique and accept that there will be many successes and many areas in which to learn and grow. You'll discover what works best and what doesn't work for you as you create each new Feng Shui Life Map and watch how the universe unfolds in response to it.

Manifesting your dream life takes just two steps: (1) Set CLEAR Intentions and SMART Goals, (2) Create reflections of these in your environment. The more you practice the principles of CLEAR and SMART, the faster you will manifest your dream life. And as you develop you skills using Feng Shui, Vision Boarding, and Creative Visualization as combined in the Feng Shui Life Mapping practice, your possibilities are endless!

It is my hope that you will feel inclined to share your successes and experiences with Feng Shui Life Mapping on Facebook: at www.Facebook.com/FengShuiLifeMapping as well as keeping in touch with me and others on my website www.FengShuiLifeMapping.com as we perfect the art of manifesting our dreams.

May you experience all the blessings of the universe!

Thank you.

Index

CPSIA information can be obtained
at www.ICGtesting.com
Printed in the USA
LVHW101715070119
603026LV00022B/1094/P